G000154426

ARCHITECTURE 10

ARCHITECTURE 10

RIBA BUILDINGS OF THE YEAR

TONY CHAPMAN

RIBA ₩ Trust

MERRELL

LONDON · NEW YORK

First published 2010 by

Merrell Publishers Limited
81 Southwark Street
London SE1 0HX

merrellpublishers.com

Text copyright © 2010 Royal Institute of British Architects
Photographs copyright © the photographers and architects;
   see individual projects and p. 271
Design and layout copyright © 2010 Merrell Publishers Limited

All rights reserved. No part of this publication may be reproduced,
stored in a retrieval system or transmitted, in any form or by any means, electronic,
mechanical, photocopying, recording or otherwise, without the prior written
permission of the publishers.

British Library Cataloguing-in-Publication Data:
Architecture 10 : RIBA buildings of the year.
1. Architecture – Awards – Great Britain – Periodicals.
2. Architecture – Awards – Europe – Periodicals.
I. Chapman, Tony, 1950– II. Royal Institute of British Architects.
720.7'941'05-dc22

ISBN 978-1-8589-4539-2

Produced by Merrell Publishers Limited
Picture research by Clemency Christopherson
Designed by Alexandre Coco
Indexed by Vicki Robinson

Printed and bound in Slovenia

THOUGHTS FROM ABROAD
TONY CHAPMAN

There is a danger in hard times that we all become more inward-looking, that we put up the shutters, hide from the world and contemplate our architectural navels. Recession is a good time for self-examination, which can be beneficial to our long-term health. Elsewhere in this book, RIBA President Ruth Reed and former Culture Secretary Lord Smith, now Chairman of the Environment Agency, consider the state of the profession in a historical context. We must not forget, however, that architecture is also an international business, and that its branches are as important as its roots.

The RIBA Lubetkin Prize is five years old. In that time it has produced winners on four continents, reflecting the huge contribution that architecture makes on the world stage. When Marco Goldschmied succeeded Jane Priestman as Chair of the RIBA Awards Group in 1996, he was determined that the new Stirling Prize should reflect the international remit of the organization and the amount of significant work being done by its members overseas. As a result, in the second year (1997) schemes anywhere in the European Union became eligible to win the prize. This system was always seen as a halfway house, since for various historical, colonial and architectural-education reasons, ever more British architecture was being built outside the EU.

And so one day in April 2005, on the 13.28 from Chelmsford to Liverpool Street, Paul Finch and I came up with the Lubetkin Prize. As I wrote in my introduction to this book in 2006, 'Stirling has a little brother: as it approaches its stroppy teens along comes the fledgling Lubetkin, mewling and puking.' Some say that it's been a sickly child ever since, and have wanted to put it out of its misery. It's not helped by the fact that many people don't know what the Lubetkin is: we've changed its rules in line with the exigencies of the architecture's geopolitics. And it's been fostered out to more than one family. The prize was first presented at the RIBA National Awards, then offered to the RIBA International Conference as a sweetener (that never happened, because the conference became a victim of the recession), and was finally made to stand on its own feet. In the future it may well find a new home. But the prize itself has gone from strength to strength, with truly internationally significant winners in the past two years.

An important part of the RIBA's remit is to reward and celebrate the work of its members overseas, not least because the RIBA has 6000 international members. Currently we achieve that goal in part through Stirling and in part through Lubetkin. However, we can never judge buildings in, say, Singapore or Uruguay (to cite two of this year's entries) with the same rigour as Stirling, which demands four stages of judging. There are other international architecture prizes that approach the problem in different ways. Our own Royal Gold Medal goes for the white-smoke approach: judges huddled in a room arguing the merits of one architect over another before releasing the news to the world.

This approach is fine, because the judges are considering a whole body of work, not a single building. Another of Paul Finch's babies, the World Architecture Festival, invites entrants to present their work to expert juries as if it were an architectural competition – another very valid way around the problem. The RIBA Lubetkin Prize holds fast to the principle that winning buildings must have been visited, and if we can't send juries of five wherever those buildings might be, we can at least send a couple of judges to see a shortlist of entries. In fact, in the first year we sent four judges, and were roundly and rightly castigated by those who were critical of the ruddy great carbon footprint we had stamped across the globe. Now just two people do the visits: the Chair of the RIBA's Awards Group and the Head of Awards – that's me. I have two qualifications: first, I am not an architect, although I've been involved in architecture for fifteen years, and every jury has a lay component; secondly, as an ex-BBC producer, I can wield a video camera and edit the results into a coherent record of the visits to show to a larger jury of three more architects, which decides the winner. In the past four years the visiting judges have only once returned to London with a firm winner in mind, and even then we were assiduous in our refusal to ram it down the throats of our fellow jurors.

On all visits, the Chair of the Awards Group wears a radio mic, and every conversation with the building's clients and architects is recorded. Given that some visits take four or five hours, that's a lot of footage. Once back home, I edit it with shots of the projects, together with plans, to make a reasonably fair record of what it was like to be there in person. Video is no more three-dimensional than still photography, yet it feels that way because the camera can explore the spaces in the same way the human eye does, zooming in, panning and taking the widest of wide shots. In addition, there's the advantage that the people are there telling the story of the building: what the brief was, how it was fulfilled (or not), what works best for the users, what doesn't (in the version the judges see, it's all there, warts and all, because clients and even sometimes the architects can be surprisingly honest about their buildings). The London judges, therefore, have a pretty fair idea about the building in use, and they use this to supplement their own assessment of the plans, which they can read in the way a musician reads a score.

This was a problematic year for the RIBA, not only for its members but also for its awards. A cloud had hung over the broadcasting of the Stirling Prize since last autumn. Getting Stirling televised, along with extending it to Europe, had been an aim of the originators of the prize back in 1996. Now Channel 4 was in some disarray, with numerous staff changes and advertising revenues slashed. The channel could not commit by the end of the year, as it had previously done. So I reopened negotiations with my old employers, the BBC. A very senior member of staff there had been courting me for some time to try to win the prize from Channel 4. I had always said we were so happy with 4's coverage of the prize that we would never walk away from them. 'What if they walked away from you?' he asked now. 'That might be different.' It is only human nature to want what you can't have, and suddenly BBC were no longer biting our hands off, but they were definitely interested. There was still no word from Channel 4, although I continued to push them. In the end the calls came through on a day when I was in Spain judging the RIBA Awards: a Chipperfield in Barcelona and a Rogers Stirk Harbour in Seville, coupled with a 'no' from Channel 4 and a 'yes' from the BBC. But could we move the prize forward by a week, and could we present it at half past six? The awards dinner had been booked for a year at the Roundhouse, and it meant being up against *Strictly Come Dancing* in the TV schedules, but hey, yes, of course we could do it. This was the BBC, a match made in Heaven with that other venerable institution, the RIBA.

It was the year of another cloud, the ash one emanating from the Icelandic volcano, of the British Airways cabin-crew strike and of revolution in Thailand, so the judging of awards in the European Union and beyond was affected. In April I was stranded in Berlin with architects Bill Taylor, former MD of Hopkins, and Cindy Walters of Walters and Cohen. We had managed to get the last flight for a week out of Heathrow on the Thursday morning, bound for Hamburg, and were due to return from Berlin on the Friday evening; it took us a further forty-eight hours. The school on the German–Danish border by Danish architects C.F. Møller was a delight – a long, low building of a creamy brick. This wasn't quite good enough to see off the two English schools that also made it to that list, but it was still very good.

By the time we had finished our visit, all flights across northern Europe were grounded. We were bound for Berlin by train, heading deeper into trouble. The next day the Neues Museum made it all worthwhile. Jaws dropped as we entered Friedrich August Stüler's masterpiece, bombed in the Second World War, unloved by the East Germans, but now rebuilt and restored by David Chipperfield and Julian Harrap. When we emerged after 5 pm, nothing was moving in the skies and every seat on every train had gone, so we had to make the most of it with an architectural tour that took in Peter Eisenman's extraordinary Holocaust Memorial; Mies van der Rohe's Neue Nationalgalerie, its marble floor covered with cheap carpets in anticipation of a hip-hop gig that evening (times are hard); and the architectural delights and horrors of Potsdamer Platz, before ending up at the bohemian Café de Paris – like the Chelsea Arts Club without the, well, Chelsea. The next day we managed to hire a car and drove to Brussels, where we stopped overnight, and then took a taxi to Calais. When we arrived, TV crews were falling over themselves to interview the few brave souls stranded there by a combination of the ash cloud and the bureaucratic refusal to allow Dan Snow's brave flotilla to rescue them and promote his latest TV documentary on, you guessed it, Dunkirk. We walked straight on to a P&O ferry instead.

The Lubetkin judging was rather more tricky. Dublin was a doddle: a day return to see the customary O'Donnell + Tuomey shortlisted scheme – some very clever housing, which looked good even on a typically soft day. The rest of the trip was round the world on nine planes and in six days (actually, it was seven days: we were crossing the International Date Line, and so I lost a day – a cause of dismay at my stage in life). Although the ash had largely subsided by May, BA cabin staff were queuing up to take its place as number-one irritant to flyers. Getting round the world without BA is harder than you might think, so it took Paul Monaghan and I twenty-five hours and three flights to reach Anchorage. It's a shame that the remnants of the ash cloud didn't drive us straight over the North Pole, because we'd have been there in seven hours. Our taxi driver was a woman who had arrived in Anchorage from Oregon when her logging village was closed down 'by the spotted owl'. Is that some kind of Neo-Con gun club? 'No, it's an owl, a protected species', she said. 'A bunch of environmentalists got all the logging stopped so that the owls were not disturbed. A thousand people used to live there, now it's seventeen.' 'Were they Californians?' I ventured. 'Sure.' 'And I bet they never even went there.' 'Too right.'

In Alaska it barely gets dark in May, June and July, nor light in winter. It was 11.30 pm and Chipperfield's Anchorage Museum looked ghostly in the half-light, or like an alien amid the undistinguished shack-like buildings and the empty lots. Most Midwestern towns look like they might once have been something; this north-western one looks like it never was. The whole thing appeared better in the sharp light of day, properly ethereal against the blue sky and the white-capped mountains, and seeming more like stainless steel than seamless glass – although, in fact, there are movement joints aplenty in this most volcanically active of states. In spite of the fact that the new landscaping had been fenced off 'to keep the moose from munching it', and despite one of the curator's lack of enthusiasm for the building's daylit spaces, we loved the museum. It shows what good architecture can do for a place, any place; it can lift the spirits and make its inhabitants feel proud. There's little else here of which to be proud. Oh, sorry, Sarah Palin, I forgot about you.

By this stage we knew that we were not going to Bangkok to see the remarkable permeable green residential tower by WOHA. The anti-government Red Shirts had been occupying the business district of the city for weeks, and on the day we flew out we were watching on TV screens at Heathrow the tanks manoeuvring into position. In fact, they cleared the demonstrators, with an admitted seventy-five deaths, the day we should have been judging. Architecture is important, but not that important, and these architects will get another chance next year. Instead we flew straight – OK, via Seattle and Seoul – to Shanghai. Time enough to write most of my 'Bluffer's Guide to Modern Architecture' for our new and extraordinarily generous sponsor, HSBC Private Bank, which has taken the RIBA Manser Medal under its wing, where it will be nurtured and will doubtless flourish. The idea of the pamphlet is to explain to HSBC's staff why, in these times, they are investing in the promotion of architecture. We could make the same case to the wider world, as it's our money too.

We were in China for a second year running, this time to see the Heatherwick Studio's spectacular UK Pavilion for the Expo 2010 Shanghai. This, we discovered, having waded our way through much architectural dross, was the star of the show by some way. The Spanish Pavilion, by Benedetta Tagliabue, was extraordinary, its shell made of thousands of basket-weave panels. It won an RIBA International Award, but was not considered to be good enough for the Lubektin shortlist by the Awards Group, who judge schemes with the aid of A1 panels and a mass of paperwork, images and plans. Now we were actually there, we were not so sure, although the pavilion's content let it down. The same could be said of the Irish Pavilion, which comprised not-bad glazed boxes full of blarney: 'Hey, did you know Bono's Irish? So was James Joyce. Guinness is too – amazing!' And the French monster: 'Did you know the tricolour's the French flag, and we make Citroëns, and our wine's rather good?' The only other pavilions that impressed me in two days of trudging round the site, visiting, judging and filming, were the Danish – a double helix of concrete ramps wrapped around the Little Mermaid (the real one) – and the Swiss – more ramps, hung with a net and red blobs, but with the best restaurant in town, where we met Thomas Heatherwick. His pavilion was dematerializing into its smoggy background when we came across it. It is intended to scotch myths about foggy days in London town and Sherlock Holmes and that it's always raining cats and dogs in the UK. Shanghai was certainly doing its best to convince us that it can rival our weather. Suggestively, not didactically, the pavilion paints a picture of a creative and cool Britain. The idea is that the half a million visitors a day, after being bombarded with videos and peering at endless unintelligible text, will appreciate the Zen calm of the Seed Cathedral. Well, everything is relative, but the excited multilingual appreciation that greeted us as we entered this sanctuary was remarkable. It almost gave one a frisson of patriotism to think that we can still do such things so well.

It may not last. The gestation time for architecture being long, we will still be seeing ripe plums on the awards tree after the 2012 Olympics. Thereafter, they may well be turning into architectural prunes. So, while we can, let's celebrate the best of British, the best of international architecture.

A YEAR IN ARCHITECTURE
RUTH REED, RIBA PRESIDENT

It would be impossible to review architecture in 2010 without reference to the economic and political upheaval of the past year. However, the resultant hiatus in construction is not only a cause for concern, but also a chance to reflect on what has been achieved in the last fifteen years of growth, before looking forward to the opportunities that may present themselves in a new political order as we climb out of recession.

If we look back to the beginning of an era of regeneration, it is possible to see that the recession of the early 1990s was a time of reflection that spawned a flowering of new thinking in architecture. Devastating as its effects were to the business of architecture, that economic downturn brought forth new talent with the establishment of new practices. There is evidence that the same is happening again: new firms have designed award-winning schemes despite a public procurement system that inhibits the work of smaller, younger practices.

Now, as the tower cranes come down and the hoardings disappear from our streets, the mass media and, by influence, the public are beginning to realize what they are missing. Architecture has garnered considerable media interest over the years, from the home-makeover shows and the *Grand Designs* TV series to the Kevin McCloud-presented Castleford Project and the RIBA Stirling Prize. The Prince of Wales continues to be an *agent provocateur* in the debate on architecture and place-making. Each intervention on his part focuses the public's mind on their image of cities and the growing acknowledgement that modern architecture has its place in our urban identity alongside our heritage. People are more aware than ever before of the benefits of investment in the built environment. New buildings and revitalized public realm reinforce civic pride and confidence in the economy, because architecture is the evidence of progress and rejuvenation. When building stops and the civic fountains are switched off, we feel devalued as a society.

Clapham Manor Primary School, London SW4, by dRMM

The recent outcry over the ending of the Building Schools for the Future (BSF) programme was notable for the nature of the voices leading the challenge to government. It was not the architects or the construction industry, both of which groups have every cause to fear the effects of a shut-down in public investment, but the teachers, heads and pupils who were appearing on our screens. The users of our schools estate are calling for society to value them enough to accommodate them in good buildings that will facilitate their learning. They can see at other schools the benefits of rebuilding and refurbishment that have improved educational performance and served the wider community. These are the lucky ones, whose projects were completed before the election. Labour politicians may have struggled during the election campaign to prove the benefits that BSF brought to people's lives, but, paradoxically, it is the cancellation of the building programme that has provided the platform to demonstrate the value of good design and captured the public imagination.

The two schools on the shortlist for the RIBA Stirling Prize in 2010 are examples of excellence and innovation in school design – a sector that, in pockets, was dramatically improving our desperately poor schools estate. Other sectors, too, have been flourishing under public patronage, most notable of which were cultural buildings. These have been the germ around which the post-industrial

John Lewis Department Store and Cineplex, Leicester, by Foreign Office Architects

cities have reinvented themselves. No longer former mill towns (or mining, steel, coal, shipbuilding or lace towns), they are now the reinvigorated 'core cities' of England and the pride of Northern Ireland, Wales and Scotland. The schemes are potent demonstrations of the wider values that good architecture creates as both physical and cultural symbols of their cities. The new galleries, theatres and arts centres have nurtured the vitality and aspirations of a growing cultured class. It is to be seen whether these institutions can now get sufficient private patronage to survive the new austerity and retain the confidence of a regional arts-led culture.

The era has also seen the revitalization of our city centres, the rebirth of an urban living that did not exist outside of London in the late twentieth century. There may well have been overkill in the provision of apartments and bars, but city living, fuelled by cultural regeneration and the rise of the cafe society, is here to stay. The return of shopping to city centres has also given them new life and new landmarks: Liverpool One, Selfridges in Birmingham and Cabot Circus in Bristol stand out as examples of good planning and great design, and in many cities new and refurbished retail centres are the weekend meccas for leisure shopping. Out-of-town units remain for the bulkier purchases, but our liberated hours now allow us to enjoy comparison shopping in cathedrals to trade. In retail, as in other commercial building, architecture is synonymous with success and prosperity.

There are other sectors that have flourished in the boom. The Accordia housing scheme in Cambridge was the culmination of an aspiration in housing, a sector that had struggled to recover from the retreat from major public provision in a market dictated by land values. Sadly, it may be the last of the great design-led schemes for some time to come. As the continuing credit squeeze limits mortgages and regional housing targets are torn up, it will be a challenge to build any housing, never mind developments with high standards of design and place-making. One paramount imperative remains, however: the urgent need to address climate change. We must not, no matter how perilous the economic situation, forsake investing in improvements to the energy efficiency of our buildings. Housing is in the front line in the race to refurbish our existing stock, and it is crucial that we find innovative and affordable high-performing housing to take us up to an 80 per cent reduction in carbon emissions by 2050.

In the new world order we need to convince everyone of the need to focus on the refurbishment of the building stock in a holistic way. If we concentrate on improving the fabric of buildings without also considering the way in which our homes will be used in the future, we will fail to realize the full potential of the stock we already have. As a predecessor of mine (Alex Gordon) so aptly said, buildings need to be long-life and loose-fit. We need to retro-fit wisely with that in mind. The physical improvements that are to be brought about need to be matched with incentives for home-owners and tenants to change their lifestyles, and so architects' understanding of the interaction of people and buildings will be essential to the development and effective use of this new wave of high-performing homes.

There are real opportunities for the profession in the rapid contraction of the state. The construction process has become heavy with legislation. There are design standards for every sector and layers of policy and regulation in the maze of approvals that litter the path to practical completion. There is now an opportunity to strip this maze back to the basic objective that lies behind all of the red tape: that of achieving the right buildings in the right place, meaning buildings that are sustainable, accessible, safe, healthy and well constructed. However, the challenge is not so much how to strip the maze back, but how to deliver the objectives with the fractured delivery mechanism that will result from localism.

The regions are no more, and in their place comes localism, a radical agenda in which communities make decisions about their future, incentivized rather than compelled by central government. This is a challenge for architecture and the RIBA as its champion. We have been used to lobbying Westminster for changes to the primary legislation and policy guidance that compels local government and other public bodies to deliver development in the built environment; now we have to court each authority with good advice and case studies to demonstrate the benefits of continuing to develop well and wisely.

We do not travel into this new battle unarmed. The RIBA awards programme has given us exemplars of every building type and the narrative of what good design can achieve. As we meet this new agenda, we should reflect on what we

Accordia, Cambridge, by Feilden Clegg Bradley Studios, Alison Brooks Architects and Maccreanor Lavington

The Centenary Building, University of Salford, Manchester, by Hodder Associates

have accomplished, and use it to illustrate the benefits and values of great design. The Stirling Prize is fifteen years old; it has seen us through this unprecedented period of economic growth and a building boom. Like back issues of the Habitat catalogue, it has tracked our changing tastes and innovations in architecture. It is a compelling argument for great design and the promotion of the genius of British architecture. The RIBA Awards that underpin Stirling are our back catalogue, tracking innovation and investment in an accessible way that can be used to convince local people they should continue to feel proud of their built environment. We can point to examples of RIBA-awarded buildings in every British town and city to make the point that great design matters to everyone and that we need to continue to invest in architecture.

Magna Science Adventure Centre, Rotherham, South Yorkshire, by Wilkinson Eyre Architects

THE RIBA STIRLING PRIZE

IN ASSOCIATION WITH THE *ARCHITECTS' JOURNAL* AND BENCHMARK

The RIBA Stirling Prize, now in its fifteenth year, is sponsored by the *Architects' Journal* and for the first time by Benchmark. It is awarded to the architects of the building thought to be the most significant for the evolution of architecture and the built environment. A building is eligible for the prize if it is in the United Kingdom or elsewhere in the European Union and is designed by a practice with a principal office in the UK. The shortlist is selected from RIBA Award-winners, and the winner receives £20,000 and a trophy designed by Morag Myerscough. The prize is named after the architect Sir James Stirling (1926–1992), one of the most important architects of his generation and a progressive thinker and designer throughout his career.

The key criterion for any award given by the RIBA is that the project should demonstrate excellence. RIBA Awards juries should assess design excellence irrespective of style, size or complexity of project. They should take into account constraints of budget, brief and timetable, and be sensitive to the economic and social contexts of each project. Juries are required to judge what they see, not what they, as architects, might have done with a similar brief. They should also understand that almost all buildings, even great works of architecture, have some flaws.

Juries are asked to judge the quality of the design of the scheme, particularly in respect of: the budget; the spatial experience that the scheme offers; the complexity of brief and degree of difficulty – the scheme's architectural ambition and ideas; its design vision; the selection and detailing of materials; the extent of innovation, invention and originality; the contract type; the appropriateness of the scheme's structural and servicing systems; fitness for purpose and the level of client satisfaction; the scheme's response to the issues of accessibility and sustainability and other social factors; its capacity to stimulate, engage and delight its occupants and visitors. An award-winning project should be capable of enduring as a fine work of architecture throughout its working life.

For previous winners of the prize, see p. 255.

WINNER

MAXXI, MUSEO NAZIONALE DELLE ARTI DEL XXI SECOLO
VIA GUIDO RENI, ROME, ITALY
ZAHA HADID ARCHITECTS

SHORTLIST

ASHMOLEAN MUSEUM OF ART AND ARCHAEOLOGY
BEAUMONT STREET, OXFORD
RICK MATHER ARCHITECTS

BATEMAN'S ROW
LONDON EC2
THEIS + KHAN ARCHITECTS

CHRIST'S COLLEGE
LARCH AVENUE, GUILDFORD
DSDHA

CLAPHAM MANOR PRIMARY SCHOOL
LONDON SW4
DRMM

NEUES MUSEUM
MUSEUMINSEL, BERLIN, GERMANY
DAVID CHIPPERFIELD ARCHITECTS IN COLLABORATION WITH JULIAN HARRAP

JUDGES

RUTH REED
RIBA PRESIDENT
RIBA President 2009–11 and Course Director of the Postgraduate Diploma in Architectural Practice at the Birmingham School of Architecture. She practised as an architect between 1992 and 2005, running Reed Architects, and is now a partner at Green Planning Solutions, a consultancy specializing in rural casework.

IVAN HARBOUR
ARCHITECT
Lead partner on two Stirling winners: Maggie's London in 2009 and Barajas Airport, Madrid, in 2006. He cut his teeth at Richard Rogers Partnership on Lloyd's of London, and led the design of the European Court of Human Rights, Strasbourg, and Bordeaux Law Courts. In 2007 the practice became Rogers Stirk Harbour + Partners in recognition of Ivan's and Graham Stirk's contributions.

EDWARD JONES
ARCHITECT
Co-founder of Dixon Jones, still best known for its remarkable work at the Royal Opera House, the National Portrait Gallery and the East Wing of the National Gallery, all in London. The practice's elegant arcade that formed part of Liverpool One was shortlisted for the Stirling Prize in 2009.

LISA JARDINE, CBE
HISTORIAN AND WRITER
Centenary Professor of Renaissance Studies at Queen Mary, University of London, and Chair of the Human Fertilisation and Embryology Authority. A patron of the Orange Prize for Fiction and a Trustee of the Victoria and Albert Museum, she is the author of a number of award-winning history books, including *Going Dutch*, which won the 2009 Cundill International Prize in History.

MARK LAWSON
BROADCASTER
RIBA Honorary Fellow and award-winning broadcaster, journalist and novelist. As presenter of the BBC's *Late Show* and later *Late Review*, and the continuing voice of Radio 4's *Front Row*, he is known for crediting his audience with at least as much intelligence as the people he is interviewing and for regularly showcasing good new architecture.

MAXXI, MUSEO NAZIONALE DELLE ARTI DEL XXI SECOLO
VIA GUIDO RENI, ROME, ITALY

ZAHA HADID ARCHITECTS

CLIENTS: MINISTERO PER I BENI E LE ATTIVITÀ CULTURALI; FONDAZIONE MAXXI;
    MINISTERO DELLE INFRASTRUTTURE E DEI TRASPORTI
STRUCTURAL ENGINEERS: STUDIO SPC; SKM ANTHONY HUNT; THE OK
    DESIGN GROUP
SERVICES ENGINEERS: MAX FORDHAM; THE OK DESIGN GROUP
CONTRACTORS: CONSORTIUM MAXXI 2006; ITALIANA COSTRUZIONI; SOCIETÀ
    APPALTI COSTRUZIONI
CONTRACT VALUE: €150,000,000
DATE OF OCCUPATION: NOVEMBER 2009
GROSS INTERNAL AREA: 21,200 SQ. M
IMAGES: IWAN BAAN (P. 19; BOTTOM; P. 22; P. 23 TOP; P. 24; P. 25); HÉLÈNE
    BINET (OPPOSITE); ROLAND HALBE (P. 23 BOTTOM)

The artist Michael Craig-Martin once said that it is the duty of the visitor to a gallery to react to the art; it is not for the artist to present everything on a plate. Zaha Hadid's MAXXI (that's Latin for 'Museum of the Art of the Twenty-first Century') responds to the dictum by challenging both visitors and curators alike. Hers is very much a twenty-first-century building in which the art comes second to the architecture, and where the responsibility is as much to the public realm as it is to the artist. MAXXI provides the neighbourhood with a piazza and makes citizens of all its visitors.

The museum is in Rome, but it does not do as the Romans do. It does not defer to the past. Because Hadid does not come from the Graeco-Roman tradition, her interests lie in the unbounded imagination, in finding new ways of thinking about space and how to contain it. The project's suburban context, with only distant glimpses of the columns and cupolas of ancient Rome, allows it a freedom denied to architects trying to build in the centre. Hadid does not mess with the Eternal City. In recent times only Richard Meier has got away with modernism there, and his riposte is polite.

The original competition-winning entry of 1999 proposed removing many but not all of the existing military buildings on the site, creating a piazza that is enclosed on three sides. The retained buildings make a quiet contrast with the structural pyrotechnics of the new design and enrich the whole composition.

Hadid has produced an object that at once challenges and intrigues; one that, far from alienating visitors, entices them in. Raked columns, like the stays on a bow-string bridge, appear to hold down the building, as well as to hold it up and announce the entrance. Once inside, the visitor is presented with a choice of sculptural objects: a white, polished-concrete amoeba of a desk; a black steel stair that staggers into space; and, in the opening exhibition at least, sculptures by Anish Kapoor that have never looked better. This is a museum of paths and routes, a museum where the curators have to be inventive in their hanging and placement of the twenty-first-century artworks that have been collected since the inception of the project. In plan, despite the drama of its exterior forms, the building is surprisingly conventional and is rationally organized as five main suites. It is the section that thrills. The whole is bravely daylit with a sinuous roof of controllable skylights, louvres and beams, while conforming to the very strict climate-control requirements of modern galleries; the skylights both orientate and excite the visitor, but also produce uplifting spaces.

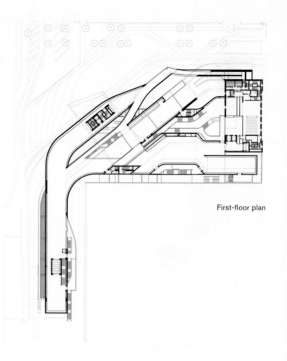

First-floor plan

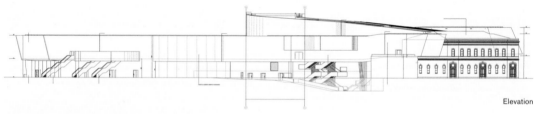

Elevation

MAXXI is described as a building for the staging of art and, while provocative on many levels, it shows a maturity and calm that belie the complexities of its form and organization. The nature of the project meant that everything had to be overspecified; throughout the design process the architect had no idea what would be hung in this series of rooms, so walls that are able to bear a tonne of rusting steel might be graced by miniatures. In use, in addition to the innovative hanging, video projections – something traditional galleries do not do well – bounce off the white curves, animating the spaces. This is great interior architecture, with form and function smoothly integrated in the way they were at Hadid's BMW factory in Leipzig (2005).

Hadid herself insists: 'You don't have to be authoritarian about what a person has to look at, or the way you look at it. This multiplied experience can be very interesting.' MAXXI is a mature piece of architecture, the distillation of years of experimentation, only a fraction of which was ever built. It is the quintessence of Hadid's constant attempt to create a landscape, a series of cavernous spaces drawn with a free, roving line. The resulting piece, rather than prescribing routes, gives the visitor a sense of exploration, as befits an art gallery (and would not suit a museum). It is probably Hadid's best work to date, and gives Rome a belief in the future to complement its pride in its past.

ASHMOLEAN MUSEUM OF ART AND ARCHAEOLOGY
BEAUMONT STREET, OXFORD

RICK MATHER ARCHITECTS

CLIENT: UNIVERSITY OF OXFORD, ASHMOLEAN MUSEUM OF ART
    AND ARCHAEOLOGY
STRUCTURAL ENGINEER: DEWHURST MACFARLANE AND PARTNERS
SERVICES ENGINEER: ATELIER TEN
EXHIBITION DESIGN: METAPHOR
CONTRACTOR: BAM CONSTRUCTION UK
CONTRACT VALUE: £62,000,000
DATE OF COMPLETION: OCTOBER 2009
GROSS INTERNAL AREA: 10,000 SQ. M
IMAGES: RICHARD BRYANT – ARCAID (P. 28; P. 29 LEFT); ANDY MATTHEWS –
    RICK MATHER ARCHITECTS (TOP; BOTTOM; OPPOSITE; P. 29 RIGHT)

The bar for this project could not have been set higher: in order
to double the display space of the oldest museum in Britain while
retaining Charles Cockerell's Grade I-listed building of 1845,
the architect was effectively required to put a ship in a bottle. The
result – 10,000 square metres of new accommodation with virtually
no external walls and largely invisible to the public realm, all built
from a single narrow access from St Giles, only a couple of metres
wide – is by no means 'mere' interior architecture. Rather, it is the
culmination of a working life spent by the architect in refining the
details of galleries, houses and restaurants to create a deeply
satisfying series of interlocking spaces.

Entered through the Cockerell façade, the new building
immediately becomes visible as the eye is drawn to a daylit space
beyond. This central atrium, modest in plan yet dramatic in its
sophisticated section, rises through six floors to create a vertical
museum. It provides an excellent quality of illumination, even on the
lower ground floor, while avoiding light levels that could damage
exhibits. The way in which the pellucid light washes through
the atrium, bathing the polished-plaster walls and hitting the

over-scaled Classical figure, lends the place a surreal quality. Critic Tom Dyckhoff has called it a building energized with light.

A subtly curved staircase – rather playful for a modernist, in the view of the RIBA President and chair of the Stirling jury, Ruth Reed – cascades down one wall, stepping outwards as it descends to produce a three-dimensional form of originality and great effect. Its raked solid balustrades are set at a different angle from the glazed balustrading, giving an orange-peel effect that adds to the beguiling composition to create what must be one of the most beautiful staircases in Britain.

The atrium is on one of the two major axes established by Cockerell, and forms part of a new and very clear route that unifies the museum and collection; the visitor never doubts his or her position in the thirty-nine new galleries. The route navigates cleverly interleaved and interconnected double- and single-height spaces (calibrated to fit the Cockerell building) in a rich spatial journey.

Complementing the clarity and ingenuity of the architecture, Stephen Greenberg (himself an architect) and his team at Metaphor have curated the displays and graphics brilliantly with the theme of 'Crossing Cultures, Crossing Time', allowing visitors to see how civilizations developed as part of an interrelated world culture. The theme is reflected in the architecture, with carefully controlled (although seemingly random) visual relationships between items in

the collection. Thus, for instance, the visitor can judge the influence of ancient Islamic ceramics on English medieval tiles with a turn of the head. Another gallery juxtaposes musical instruments with the rugs that would have carpeted the rooms in which they were played. Most of the display cases are free-standing and beautifully detailed. Others are non-existent, allowing the visitor the pleasure of being able to walk around a bronze or a stone statue, his or her view unimpeded by reflections – something few galleries dare to do. There are no whizzy graphics: the curators state confidently that video displays have had their day, and certainly they do date expensively and quickly. Instead, the objects and the relationships between them form a three-dimensional website that can be inhabited, not merely browsed. No more than 1 per cent of the museum's collections are on display, but the creation of two excellent temporary galleries mitigate this statistic. As well as the galleries, the building provides the usual public facilities: a new education centre, conservation studios and a rooftop restaurant with a terrace giving wonderful views across the spires of Oxford.

The director of the museum, Dr Christopher Brown, asserts: 'This is Rick Mather's finest building to date, and I have no doubt that it'll be recognized very soon as one of the outstanding museum buildings of the twenty-first century.' A tour de force of ingenuity, restraint, invention and tact, this is indeed a world-class building.

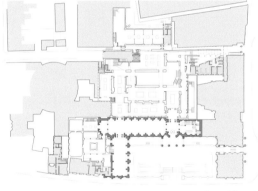

Ground-floor plan

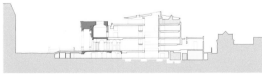

Section

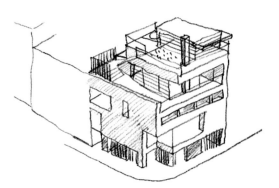

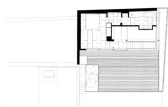

Fourth-floor plan

Third-floor plan

Second-floor plan

First-floor plan

Ground-floor plan

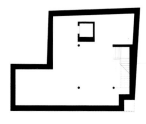

Basement plan

BATEMAN'S ROW
LONDON EC2

THEIS + KHAN ARCHITECTS

CLIENTS: SORAYA KHAN AND PATRICK THEIS
STRUCTURAL ENGINEER: F.J. SAMUELY AND PARTNERS
CONTRACTOR: SILVER INTERIORS DESIGN & BUILD
CONTRACT VALUE: £1,600,000
DATE OF COMPLETION: SEPTEMBER 2009
GROSS INTERNAL AREA: 867 SQ. M
IMAGES: NICK KANE – ARCAID
SHORTLISTED FOR THE RIBA MANSER MEDAL

This ambitious and complex building, achieved on and maximizing an unprepossessing corner site, represents a fine piece of urban dentistry. It is a clever, economically sustainable six-storey development by an architect-client couple, encompassing a mix of uses, including their home and office. An exercise in architectural self-sufficiency, the building contains four dwellings (an apartment on three floors, two flats stacked in a mews house, and a small studio flat), the architects' own studio on the first floor and a private art gallery on the ground floor and basement.

In effect, these enterprising architect-developers live above the shop. The floor heights are cleverly adjusted throughout, creating taller spaces for the gallery in the basement, the studio on the first floor and the principal living space on the third floor. Bedrooms for the family flat and the small studio flat are on the second floor. Over the six storeys the floor-to-ceiling heights alternate between 12 and 8 feet (3.7 and 2.4 metres), adding to the richness of the experience as you climb the building, whether by the clever dual-access lift – which allows use only by those authorized so to do – or by means of the castle-like spiral stair. The studio, the gallery and the flats have separate stairs and entrances from the street, but are all connected by the same lift.

The architects sold their home and borrowed heavily to finance this brave project, which was designed to pay for itself. In effect, the loan required them to rent out at least half of the property. So they dug down 3 metres to gain rentable space and spent three years negotiating with the landlord to exchange rights of light via three windows to his neighbouring property for a small parcel of land, for which they agreed to design a mews house to match their own. With a gallery taking the ground and lower ground floors and tenants the flats, it has all worked out beautifully.

A base of dark, vertically laid brick defines the back-of-pavement of the narrow streets. For the first floor and above, the architects sought a Suffolk white brick to match that used in a number of nearby Edwardian buildings (many of them once small furniture factories), but found the seam had long been exhausted. Instead, they chose a pale, creamy Danish brick with a flush mortar, which contributes a somewhat ethereal quality to the mundane surroundings. In terms of construction, the building becomes progressively lighter towards the top, and there is an American quality to the living room and terraces on the top floors, which provide impressive views of the City of London. The scheme even has its own High Line – although, unlike in New York, it is

still a working London Overground line, with trains sliding past the third floor.

In its response to its surroundings, its scale and its mix of uses, this development defines a vision for the future of Shoreditch, a part of London that has fully embraced the rich variety of functions embodied in the building. It provides an environment for family living within a tough urban context and a flat with qualities that could not easily be found in a house. It has a fortress-like quality, towering over the hubbub that is Shoreditch on weekend evenings, providing a safe haven and respite for the couple and their children.

At no point during the lengthy process of realizing the project – ten years from first negotiations with adjoining owners and the raising of funds to build it – was there a loss of ambition. No corners were cut, and the resulting house seems to be the product of a far more generous budget than the one it enjoyed. The architects have found a way of developing a tight, difficult site in a way that is both spatially and aesthetically rich.

This is a great city-making building, executed with extraordinary care and judgement, with the type of scale and mix that is simultaneously ordinary and relevant. London and the depressed housing market require far more of its kind.

CHRIST'S COLLEGE
LARCH AVENUE, GUILDFORD

DSDHA

CLIENTS: DIOCESE OF GUILDFORD; SURREY COUNTY COUNCIL
LANDSCAPE ARCHITECT: TOWNSHEND LANDSCAPE ARCHITECTS
STRUCTURAL ENGINEER: ADAMS KARA TAYLOR
SERVICES ENGINEER: ATELIER TEN
PROJECT AND COST MANAGER: DAVIS LANGDON
CONTRACTOR: WATES CONSTRUCTION
CONTRACT VALUE: £14,400,000
DATE OF OCCUPATION: JANUARY 2009
GROSS INTERNAL AREA: 7350 SQ. M
IMAGES: HÉLÈNE BINET (BOTTOM; OPPOSITE); DENNIS GILBERT – VIEW
    (P. 36; P. 37)
SHORTLISTED FOR THE RIBA SORRELL FOUNDATION SCHOOLS AWARD

This school does not look as though it belongs in Guildford, or even in Britain. Rather, we might be in Switzerland or Scandinavia, where good architecture has long been a prerequisite for good education. With its generous approach and its dark-brown brick elevations, the building stands as a beacon for an all-too-shortlived commitment to the notion that high design quality produces better places in which children can learn and develop.

This clever design for a secondary school is a worthy companion to the adjoining special-needs school by the same architect, winner of an RIBA Award in 2009. But whereas that was

Section

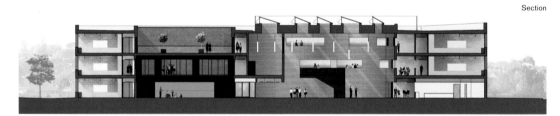

a single storey, as befits a building for young people with real learning and physical difficulties, the new school works on three compact levels, yet has a gratifying generosity of circulation and inner courtyard spaces.

As judge Edward Jones pointed out, at first sight the chosen *parti* seems an odd one for the suburban setting. The defensive wall surrounding an enclosed atrium is perhaps more suited to city block than greenfield site. But even Guildford has its more troubled quarters, and vandalism and bullying were endemic in the old school. Furthermore, there have been two arson attacks in the past three years, so this robust response to the problem of providing secure accommodation in a tough area is a wholly appropriate one.

The building has an innovative natural ventilation system, which works well on the hottest of summer days and is subtly manifested on the deep-brown brickwork as occasional patterns of gaps in the pointing. The fenestration is equally handsomely arranged in each façade, has deep reveals, and in places accentuates key views across Guildford. One tall window, which illumines a stairwell, contains one of the biggest single pieces of glass available in the United Kingdom. Although the school cost less than £2000 per square metre, such details demonstrate that nowhere have corners noticeably been cut.

The five faculties within the school are boldly identified with brightly coloured doors, in a predominantly grey, black and concrete series of internal finishes, which are subtle, grown-up and calming. No wonder the students' behaviour has been positively modified by the building, which gives them a sense of responsibility and ownership; all the pupils seem older than their years. The atrium at the centre of the school has to perform many functions, something

it does flexibly and with ease, and it is a focus for the school community. It also allows passive surveillance of pupils by their peers and teachers. There is nothing heavy-handed here; it is all too open for that. Walls and ceilings are lined in cheap pine boards, yet because of the quality of the design the space is not sauna-like. Although it is an internal space, it is illuminated evenly by large rooflights. The tables at one edge of the space accommodate computers for informal teaching; other dining tables can be swept away to allow trampolining or other games – although there is a splendid, robust, daylit gym elsewhere. The atrium is, however, primarily a meeting place, a big, generous, warm room that is the true heart of a fine building.

The classrooms are sturdy, functional spaces that are constantly being adapted to the requirements of the everyday life of the school. Many are dual-aspect, and all enjoy good light levels and fine views. The old school – now demolished and the site of new playing fields – was a muddle of the kinds of buildings that accrete everywhere on school campuses over time; the new one has a unity of design and purpose, and looks as if it should stand the test of time.

While many are following the happy-clappy route of school design, the architects have chosen another way, undoubtedly inspired by their Swiss teaching experience but informed by a growing understanding of the needs of British schoolchildren, who were so woefully served by politicians and many architects in the later part of the twentieth century. This is a mature piece that will help its pupils to mature into well-rounded adults. It would be tragic if these efforts are stymied by the current economic climate and our response to it.

CLAPHAM MANOR PRIMARY SCHOOL
LONDON SW4

DRMM

CLIENT: LAMBETH AMPD
STRUCTURAL ENGINEER: MICHAEL HADI ASSOCIATES
SERVICES ENGINEER: FULCRUM CONSULTING
CONTRACTOR: THE CONSTRUCTION PARTNERSHIP
CONTRACT VALUE: £2,500,000
DATE OF COMPLETION: SEPTEMBER 2009
GROSS INTERNAL AREA: 927 SQ. M
IMAGES: JONAS LENCER
SHORTLISTED FOR THE RIBA SORRELL FOUNDATION SCHOOLS AWARD

This jewel-like project represents a very particular approach to the problem of how to improve the learning and teaching environments of the next generation. A free-standing addition to a nineteenth-century London Board school, it (in the words of the architect) 'plugs into' the existing school building to form a single entity. Too many of these fine old buildings have been wastefully demolished when they can be made to work, both environmentally and spatially. This project demonstrates how.

Clapham Manor is an antidote to the belief, common in government today, that kids can be well taught in disused DIY stores. The multicoloured glass cladding, which is the first thing to strike the viewer, gave one of the Stirling judges, Mark Lawson, broadcaster and a parent-governor, his one and only 'Prince Charles moment'. Why stick a Rubik's cube next to a red-brick building? But he was quickly won over: the colour is crucial, it excites children, and they respond positively to it. As the architect Sadie Morgan says, 'Children have this wonderful, unselfconscious love of colour.' Moreover, it soon became evident that this is no straightforward glass box. Despite the use of a repetitive modular façade system, the new intervention is actually very intimate in scale. For once, a building delivers more in reality than its published images would suggest. The panels, although all glazed externally, are internally variously transparent, translucent and opaque. As well as greatly improving the energy performance of the building, this arrangement allows teachers to attach work to the coloured pinboard lining panels. It also affords a degree of privacy and intimacy.

The building forms a simple rectangle in the gap between two existing buildings, and its diagonal relation to the existing school has created space for a transparent atrium that separates old and new. This volume cleverly handles the changes in level between the two parts of the school, the newer of which manages to achieve the added value of an extra storey. It works visually from the street because the floors are disguised by the smooth glass skin. The newness and modernity of the proposal give the project a non-institutional lightness of touch. The façade system allows good light and views at different heights for children and adults, and the use of coloured panels, in what one commentator has called 'boisterous polychromy', gives the scheme a singular identity. Far from patronizing its neighbours, the building enlivens them. It produced virtually no opposition from local residents at the planning stage, and they are proud of it in use. Stirling judge Ivan Harbour said of the school: 'Like all good pieces of architecture, it does something beyond its boundaries. It's sorted out an old back alley and made a wonderful new front door. It's made a positive contribution to the public realm.'

Section

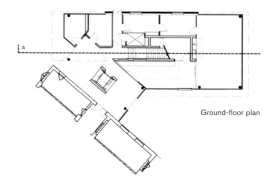

Ground-floor plan

The angled geometry of the extension also provides a very successful and secure entry sequence, with a visitors' holding point, a highly visible school office and a reception space. It is an extremely adult approach.

Internally, there are no corridors; one accesses the classrooms either through the adjoining spaces or from the central gallery leading from the atrium. All internal spaces are finished to a very high standard, with perforated acoustic panelling throughout (timber for the walls and fibreboard for the ceilings) acting as a unifying surface.

The project is a remarkably inventive and uplifting example of what the next generation of school buildings could be. It avoids generic solutions and uses the very best contemporary thinking about what makes a good educational environment. Every project needs its champion in order for the architect to realize his or her vision, and at Clapham Manor the head teacher has proved to be a man whose aesthetic judgement matches his clear educational vision. The scheme acts as an exemplar for the way in which the ambitious but ill-fated Building Schools for the Future programme might have transformed schools' building stock in Britain.

NEUES MUSEUM
MUSEUMINSEL, BERLIN, GERMANY

DAVID CHIPPERFIELD ARCHITECTS IN COLLABORATION
WITH JULIAN HARRAP

CLIENT: STIFTUNG PREUSSISCHER KULTURBESITZ
STRUCTURAL ENGINEER: INGENIEURGRUPPE BAUEN
SERVICES ENGINEER: JMP
QUANTITY SURVEYOR: NANNA FÜTTERER FOR DAVID CHIPPERFIELD
    ARCHITECTS
CONTRACTOR: BUNDESAMT FÜR BAUWESEN UND RAUMORDNUNG
CONTRACT VALUE: €200,000,000
DATE OF OCCUPATION: OCTOBER 2009
GROSS INTERNAL AREA: 20,500 SQ. M
IMAGES: JÖRG VON BRUCHHAUSEN (OPPOSITE, TOP RIGHT AND BOTTOM);
    CHRISTIAN RICHTERS – VIEW (TOP; P. 45); UTE ZSCHARNT (BOTTOM;
    OPPOSITE, TOP LEFT; P. 44)
WINNER OF THE CROWN ESTATE CONSERVATION AWARD; SEE PP. 81–83

The Neues Museum was designed by Friedrich August Stüler, and built between 1841 and 1859 to show off the archaeological and scientific prowess of one of Europe's leading powers. In a way, it was Prussia's answer to Britain's Great Exhibition of 1851.

Extensive bombing during the Second World War left the building in ruins, with entire sections completely destroyed and others severely damaged. Life under the DDR was harsh for the building: few attempts were made to repair the structure, much of which was left exposed to the elements. Despite threats to demolish it completely, and through its ingenious use as a repository, it survived, and in 1997 an international architectural competition was held for its restoration. It is the third project to be completed on Museum Island, and forms the latest addition to a masterplan that will eventually see all the museums linked. A new entrance building, also designed by Chipperfield and currently under construction on

Section

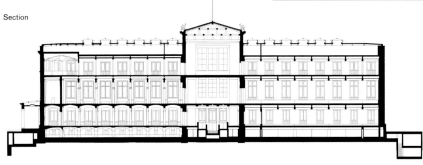

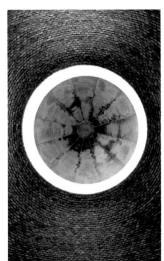

an adjacent site, will provide extra cafe and retail space for the campus and will unify the whole.

The museum houses Egyptian and prehistoric/early archaeological collections, and is a centre for active scientific research as well as public dissemination. This duality lay at the heart of the organization of the project. A unique integration of client and science, together with a close collaboration between Chipperfield and that most meticulous of conservation architects, Julian Harrap, has resulted in an exceptionally coherent, holistic piece of architecture.

The key architectural aim was to reinstate the original volumes and repair the parts remaining after the war. The restoration philosophy follows the guidelines laid down in the Charter of Venice respecting the historic structure in its different states of 'as found' preservation. Stirling judge and historian Lisa Jardine described the work in critical (not architectural) terms as 'postmodern' in that it detaches elements of the building from their environment, allowing them to be admired as fragments. The original structure and decoration are emphasized in terms of spatial context and materiality, but repairs and restoration respond in a clearly articulated but sensitive manner. There is no mere pastiche. The same archaeological approach has been applied outside and within. Elevationally, the rebuilt wing and one corner are done in plain, randomly coloured and laid recycled bricks, with windows mirroring, although not slavishly copying, the originals.

The insertion and integration of a new interior and museum environment have been impeccably judged, the cool modernism a perfect foil to both the exuberant invention of Stüler and the ancient objects on display. The new spaces are tranquil, demonstrating a coherent architectural expression through a controlled palette of materials and detailing. Pre-cast concrete is the principal structural medium, and the overall result is one of consistency, high quality and understated beauty. Nothing is left to chance; there are no forgotten or unloved corners. This is a museum of architectural history as much as one of archaeology.

The integration into the historic fabric of the lighting, air, power and safety systems needed for a contemporary museum is exemplary, and the work of just one of the project architects. Each space was considered as a mini design project in its own right, and services were introduced into damaged areas before they were repaired.

The museum directorate laudably resisted the temptation to present the visitor with too many exhibits. Less is indeed more in both the architecture and the display, providing lessons for other museums and galleries. The museum director wanted his prize exhibit, the bust of Nefertiti, to be placed at the top of the main stair, but the architect held out for the architectural purity of this major space. The bust is housed instead in a room that might have been designed for it: a small, dark octagon lit only by a rooflight. The rebuilt corner of the museum, meanwhile, culminates in a double-height gallery with a brick dome illuminated by a rooflight – a latter-day Pantheon.

As befits a museum of this stature, this is the project of a lifetime for all concerned. It is an extraordinary achievement and a creative fusion of new and old.

THE RIBA
LUBETKIN PRIZE

The RIBA Lubetkin Prize is awarded to the architect of the best RIBA International Award-winning building. Buildings eligible for RIBA International Awards are those outside the European Union or those built in the EU (with the exception of the United Kingdom) that are designed by a practice based outside the UK.

The prize is named after Berthold Lubetkin (1901–1990), the architect from Georgia who immigrated to Britain in the 1930s and went on to establish the radical architecture group Tecton. He is best known for the two Highpoint buildings in Highgate, London (1933–38), and for the Penguin Pool at London Zoo (1934). The pool provided the inspiration for a cast-concrete plaque designed and made by the artist Petr Weigl. The plaque was presented to the winner of the Lubetkin Prize by Lubetkin's daughter Sasha at a ceremony in June 2010 at the RIBA supported by UK Trade & Investment.

For previous winners of the prize, see p. 255.

WINNER

UK PAVILION, EXPO 2010 SHANGHAI
SHANGHAI, CHINA
HEATHERWICK STUDIO

SHORTLIST

ANCHORAGE MUSEUM AT
RASMUSON CENTER
ANCHORAGE, ALASKA,
UNITED STATES
DAVID CHIPPERFIELD ARCHITECTS

TIMBERYARD SOCIAL HOUSING
CORK STREET, DUBLIN, IRELAND
O'DONNELL + TUOMEY

VISITING JUDGES

PAUL MONAGHAN
CHAIR OF THE RIBA AWARDS GROUP

TONY CHAPMAN
RIBA HEAD OF AWARDS

FULL JURY

RUTH REED
RIBA PRESIDENT

KEITH WILLIAMS
ARCHITECT, KEITH WILLIAMS
ARCHITECTS

PAUL FINCH
EDITORIAL DIRECTOR OF THE
ARCHITECTS' JOURNAL AND
CHAIR OF CABE

UK PAVILION, EXPO 2010 SHANGHAI
SHANGHAI, CHINA

HEATHERWICK STUDIO

CLIENT: FOREIGN AND COMMONWEALTH OFFICE
STRUCTURAL ENGINEER: ADAMS KARA TAYLOR
ENVIRONMENTAL ENGINEER: ATELIER TEN
EXHIBITION DESIGN (WALKWAY): TROIKA
CONTENT ADVISERS: MARK JONES; JOHN SORRELL
CONTRACTOR: MACE
CONTRACT VALUE: £13,500,000
DATE OF OCCUPATION: MAY 2010
GROSS INTERNAL AREA: 1500 SQ. M
IMAGES: HEATHERWICK STUDIO

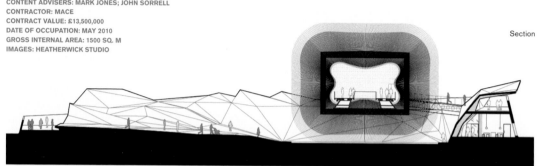

Section

Some 60,000 fibre-optic rods, each 7.5 metres long and each containing a seed, make up the Seed Cathedral, the UK Pavilion at Expo 2010 Shanghai. The seeds, all different, come from the Kunming Institute of Botany, China's equivalent of the Millennium Seed Bank at the Royal Botanic Gardens, Kew. The surrounding public space, a prime, 6000-square-metre plot by the Huangpu River, takes its inspiration from a sheet of crumpled paper (in fact, it is glass fibre, the red-flecked, pale grey of which picks up on the colours of the pavilion itself). The space is a place of rest and relative calm amid the hubbub of the rest of the Expo site: people sit in their hundreds on the 'grass' – something they cannot do anywhere else in China – and stare in wonder at the Seed Cathedral, or have their photographs taken in front of it. The brief called for a structure that offers a 'bold and lasting vision of the UK as a creative, innovative and exciting country', so the pavilion also has the job of showcasing Britain as a place that is worthy of investment and of visiting or studying in. It was required to be both iconic and practical, and to feature in the top-five Expo attractions – an aim that it has more than surpassed.

Heatherwick Studio's architectural response to this interesting brief is at once subtle and showy: subtle in that, unlike most of the 239 other pavilions, this one is not full of throbbing video screens and flashing lights; showy in that by day it resembles a giant sea urchin whose spines suck the daylight inside, while by night, with the LED light sources activated, it glows and entices visitors within.

A prettier and perhaps more appropriate analogy – because the UK takes the future of the planet very seriously, but does not resort to preaching on the subject – is with a dandelion clock flitting across the ground. Even the three exhibitions that are embedded in the overhang of the pavilion's base, and which mark the route to and from the Seed Cathedral, are more playful than didactic. They celebrate the Expo's theme of green cities, with displays showing the amount of green space in the UK's capital cities, its diverse building types (in acrylic), and samples of the plants that might safeguard all our futures. Local guides offer ad hoc commentaries here and inside the Seed Cathedral. Housed underneath the grey ground, out of public view, are all the neutral spaces required by government, sponsors and administrators – an arrangement that suits all.

The pavilion's special quality lies in the way in which the outside is carried through to the inside. It is one idea and one material, and is all the more powerful for that. The building is its content; the content is the building. This kind of claim is normally an empty conceit, but the artist in Heatherwick makes it work. He also avoided the common problem of exhibition structures: nice building, shame about the contents. This is low-tech, monochrome and silent – a subtle understatement about Britain.

The structure is timber. Back in the UK, a five-axis computer-controlled drilling machine made the holes in the plywood panels in exactly the right places and at the right angles. The rods – hollow aluminium tipped at either end with acrylic – were also cut off-site and the whole lot shipped to China to be assembled on-site. The

trades had to be taught on the job, but the process went so well that the pavilion was ready ahead of schedule and has given Britain something else to boast about at this extraordinary Expo. When the Chinese government rang to congratulate David Cameron on becoming prime minister, they told him how impressed they were by the UK Pavilion. It is entirely appropriate for an exhibition building to be a one-liner, an object building; that is how it becomes a talking point. And every one of the Expo's 90 million visitors will have had something to talk about, even if they have not been inside the pavilion. This one has walked straight into the history books, and even if it were not to survive, it will always be remembered.

ANCHORAGE MUSEUM AT RASMUSON CENTER
ANCHORAGE, ALASKA, UNITED STATES

DAVID CHIPPERFIELD ARCHITECTS

ARCHITECT OF RECORD: KUMIN ASSOCIATES
CLIENT: ANCHORAGE MUSEUM AT RASMUSON CENTER
STRUCTURAL ENGINEER: MAGNUSSON KLEMENCIC ASSOCIATES
STRUCTURAL ENGINEER OF RECORD: BBFM ENGINEERS
SERVICES ENGINEERS: AFFILIATED ENGINEERS NW; RSA ENGINEERING
FAÇADE CONSULTANT: W.J. HIGGINS & ASSOCIATES
CONTRACTOR: ALCAN GENERAL
CONTRACT VALUE: $39,705,000
DATE OF OCCUPATION: MAY 2009
GROSS INTERNAL AREA: 8404 SQ. M
IMAGES: CHRISTIAN RICHTERS – VIEW

Section

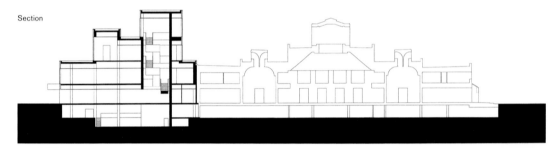

David Chipperfield Architects' latest American building is the most remote from Europe. With its vertically fritted mirror-glass façade, it looks like rectilinear blocks of ice cut from the mountains that loom over the city of Anchorage.

There are five such blocks of differing heights, depths, breadths and volumes. Glass forms an apparently seamless skin, although there are movement joints aplenty, both horizontal and vertical, in this the most seismically active state in the Union. It covers all of the façades but is only 30 per cent transparent, offering tantalizing, distorted views of what is going on inside and mirroring the dramatically changing quality and clarity of light across the seasons. The result – in this matter-of-fact, architecturally mundane city – is ethereal and extraordinarily beautiful. Seldom has a new piece of architecture so transformed not only the building it extends and makes sense of, but also the city it graces.

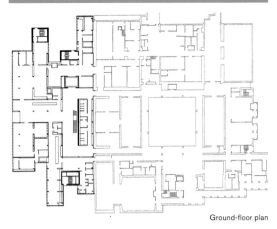

Ground-floor plan

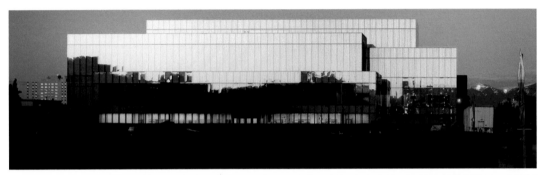

The visitor enters a ground floor that is more about community use than it is about displaying the collections of the region's cultural treasures. Internally, this is the kind of architecture on which Chipperfield cut his teeth: sharp, functional fit-outs, an all-white shop and an all-red restaurant. The building also houses the Resource Center, a temporary exhibition gallery and the Smithsonian Arctic Studies Center; there is no mistaking where we are.

In section, there is a clear pyramidical arrangement, with the public-facing facilities spreading out to give a street presence to the museum, a top-floor glass box for display and a viewing platform for the panorama of snow-capped black mountains.

Chipperfield wanted to build here because there was no competition, no context, save for the surrounding natural wonders. It seems likely that in time this fine building will have the regenerative effect expected of it, and that the 'Anchorage effect' will come to mean the siting in a city in need of TLC of a major piece of architecture that reflects the best qualities of that place back to it, instead of demanding to be looked at for its cleverness.

N READING ROOM

TIMBERYARD SOCIAL HOUSING
CORK STREET, DUBLIN, IRELAND

O'DONNELL + TUOMEY

CLIENT: DUBLIN CITY COUNCIL
STRUCTURAL ENGINEER: DOWNES ASSOCIATES
SERVICES ENGINEER: BURO HAPPOLD
CONTRACTOR: TOWNLINK CONSTRUCTION
CONTRACT VALUE: €12,500,000
DATE OF OCCUPATION: SEPTEMBER 2009
AREA: 3807 SQ. M
IMAGES: DENNIS GILBERT – VIEW

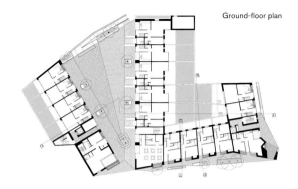

Ground-floor plan

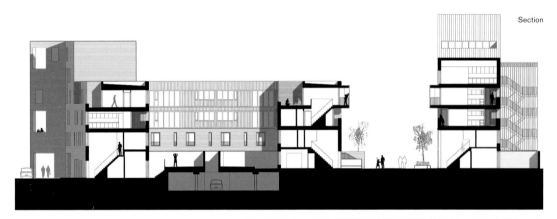

Section

When a small tear was made in the urban fabric of Dublin by the construction of the Coombe bypass, O'Donnell + Tuomey came up with a way of repairing it with a highly modulated wall of housing that is almost Byker-like in its form and impact. The sculptural wall is broken up with deep-set windows or blind cuts, by setbacks to create terraces and by the vertical use of iroko timber in screens. The building line cranks to hug the street, and at ground level there are built-in granite planters-cum-seats (first used in the firm's small terrace of housing in the village of Galbally, County Limerick). These features, and the fact that the lower flats open straight on to the street, encourage a sense of community and mitigate against the impact of the project on the neighbouring two-storey housing. The scheme is also polite in the way it steps down towards these houses from the six-storey volumes at the front, which take their scale from the industrial buildings across the road.

To deliver an urban idea with social housing is a great achievement. The main communal space is an open-ended wedge,

passively surveyed by the residents whose flats overlook it. Here children play happily and apparently safely just metres from a busy main road. The nanny state is entirely absent. These are grown-up spaces in which to grow up, and this is a country with a post-recession future that is surely all the brighter for the talents that the likes of O'Donnell + Tuomey bring to its architecture.

Gratifyingly, the interiors match up to the quality of the external detailing; indeed, all the same materials are used for the inside–outside staircases and the interiors: iroko, steel, concrete and glass. There is a materiality and a tactile quality that speak volumes of the architect pair's education at the feet of James Stirling. This is rigour delivered with love. Shrinking budgets for housing in Ireland and the UK may well mean that we will not see the scheme's like again for some time, but the delivered ambition will remain as a beacon for the way people can and should be housed decently and in well-designed spaces.

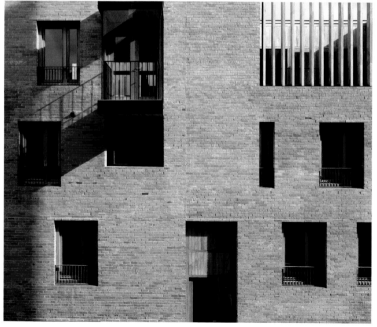

THE RIBA
INTERNATIONAL AWARDS

Buildings eligible for the RIBA International
Awards are those outside the European Union or
those built in the EU (with the exception of the
United Kingdom) that are designed by a practice
based outside the UK. The awards are judged by
members of the Awards Group, who carefully
consider the entry material. A shortlist for the
Lubetkin Prize is then drawn up, and shortlisted
schemes are visited.

JUDGES

PAUL MONAGHAN (CHAIR)
BOB ALLIES
GIANNI BOTSFORD
ALISON BROOKS
TONY CHAPMAN
PETER CLEGG
TOM DYCKHOFF
PAUL FINCH
MURRAY FRASER
RICHARD GRIFFITHS
PHILIP GUMUCHDJIAN
FARSHID MOUSSAVI
DEBORAH SAUNT
BILL TAYLOR
CINDY WALTERS

AEROPUERTO INTERNACIONAL DE CARRASCO
MONTEVIDEO, URUGUAY

RAFAEL VIÑOLY ARCHITECTS

CLIENT: PUERTA DEL SUR
STRUCTURAL ENGINEERS: THORNTON TOMASETTI; MAGNONE-POLLIO
SERVICES ENGINEERS: LUIS LAGOMARSINO & ASSOCIATES; JACK JAFFE
CONTRACTOR: CAMPIGLIA CONSTRUCCIONES
CONTRACT VALUE: CONFIDENTIAL
DATE OF OCCUPATION: NOVEMBER 2009
GROSS INTERNAL AREA: 42,719 SQ. M
IMAGES: DANIELA MAC ADDEN

It is appropriate that Uruguay's first truly international airport has been designed by its first truly international architect. What has emerged is a building that can take its place in the long tradition of airport structures – from Eero Saarinen's TWA building in New York onwards – that are abstract representations of flight.

It is this simple yet finely detailed white arched wing, 365 metres in length, that provides the building with its architectural iconography and gives it its character. Above and below, the curved steel structure is clad in reflective white fabric, stretched taut as it was on early lightweight flying machines – a fabric that glistens and reflects solar radiation back at the sky as well as bouncing daylight deep into the building.

Section

BRAS BASAH MASS RAPID TRANSIT STATION
SINGAPORE

WOHA

CLIENT: LAND TRANSPORT AUTHORITY
STRUCTURAL ENGINEERS: MAUNSELL CONSULTANTS (SINGAPORE)
    WITH WORLEY PARSONS
ACOUSTICS CONSULTANT: ACVIRON ACOUSTICS
LANDSCAPE CONSULTANT: CICADA
CONTRACTOR: WOH HUP-SHANGHAI TUNNEL ENGINEERING CO.
CONTRACT VALUE: S$75,000,000
DATE OF OCCUPATION: APRIL 2009
GROSS INTERNAL AREA: 16,289,607 SQ. M
IMAGES: PATRICK BINGHAM-HALL (TOP; BOTTOM RIGHT); TIM GRIFFITH –
    ARCAID (BOTTOM LEFT)

Bras Basah brilliantly and beautifully solves two architectural conundrums: how to give an underground station above-ground presence, and how to get daylight deep into the station. A vast glazed rooflight is covered by a pool that reflects an image of the curved façade of the colonial Singapore Art Museum; it is skylight, landscape and art rolled into one elegant object.

    The pool also forms part of the environmental strategy. The water absorbs heat from the station, which is released as it cascades over the pool edge into fountains, evaporating and thereby cooling the gardens. Frits on the glass help to prevent solar gain.

Section

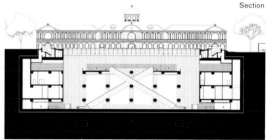

HERNING MUSEUM OF CONTEMPORARY ART
HERNING, DENMARK

STEVEN HOLL ARCHITECTS WITH KJAER & RICHTER

CLIENT: HOLGER REENBERG
STRUCTURAL ENGINEER: NIRAS
SERVICES ENGINEERS: NIRAS; TRANSSOLAR
CONTRACTOR: C.C. CONTRACTOR
CONTRACT VALUE: CONFIDENTIAL
DATE OF OCCUPATION: AUGUST 2009
GROSS INTERNAL AREA: 5600 SQ. M
IMAGES: IWAN BAAN

RIBA International Fellow Steven Holl's latest museum brings together three distinct cultural institutions and combines music with the visual arts. The design of this ground-hugger was inspired by the shirts that used to be made on the site, appearing from the air as a pile of randomly flailing shirt sleeves. In fact, it is a complex spatial composition that ties the buildings into their dramatic, bermed landscape setting. The mounds and pools conceal parking and services, with the pools also reflecting the beauty of the geometries of the structures.

While the exteriors are all about form and mass, the interiors are concerned with light and space. Curved roof sections flood the galleries with daylight, and the walls are lightweight and easily movable. Jutland is rightly proud of its new regional arts centre.

South elevation

West elevation

KROON HALL, SCHOOL OF FORESTRY & ENVIRONMENTAL STUDIES, YALE UNIVERSITY
NEW HAVEN, CONNECTICUT, UNITED STATES

HOPKINS ARCHITECTS

CLIENT: YALE UNIVERSITY
STRUCTURAL ENGINEER: ARUP
SERVICES ENGINEERS: ARUP; ATELIER TEN
CONTRACTOR: TURNER CONSTRUCTION COMPANY
CONTRACT VALUE: $33,500,000
DATE OF OCCUPATION: MAY 2009
GROSS INTERNAL AREA: 6208 SQ. M
IMAGES: MORLEY VON STERNBERG – ARCAID

Hopkins's Kroon Hall brings a touch of Cambridge UK to Yale USA. As befits a building for a school of environmental studies, it achieved an LEED Platinum rating, scoring 59 out of 60. And the use of red oak from Yale's own forests should keep the School of Forestry happy.

Internally, there are no 'neutral' spaces: everywhere you are aware of the external form. In effect, it is a giant piece of furniture, an impression enhanced by the timber linings; the exposed, arched, laminated Douglas fir roof beams; and the screens, which echo the louvres. The result is an environment that is at once comfortable and studious; a healthy and supportive environment for work and study. The scheme sets a benchmark not only for Yale but also for the whole country.

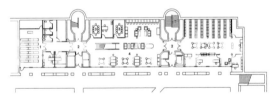

Ground-floor plan

MARGOT AND BILL WINSPEAR OPERA HOUSE
DALLAS, TEXAS, UNITED STATES

FOSTER + PARTNERS
WITH KENDALL/HEATON ASSOCIATES

CLIENT: AT&T PERFORMING ARTS CENTER
STRUCTURAL ENGINEERS: BURO HAPPOLD; THORNTON TOMASETTI
SERVICES ENGINEERS: BATTLE MCCARTHY; CHP & ASSOCIATES
THEATRE CONSULTANT: THEATRE PROJECTS
ACOUSTICS CONSULTANT: SOUND SPACE DESIGN
LIGHTING CONSULTANT: CLAUDE R. ENGLE
ACCESS CONSULTANT: PIELOW FAIR
CONTRACTOR: LINBECK
CONTRACT VALUE: CONFIDENTIAL
DATE OF OCCUPATION: OCTOBER 2009
GROSS INTERNAL AREA: 21,775 SQ. M
IMAGES: NIGEL YOUNG – FOSTER + PARTNERS

At Dallas, Foster + Partners has developed a new paradigm, with the opera house itself becoming part of the urban landscape. The auditorium, with its curvilinear form clad in rich, red glass, is visible from afar. The foyer is fully glazed, and the spiralling grand staircase leading up to the balconies provides a theatrical experience for the city as well as the opera-goers.

In order to prevent solar gain, the oversailing canopy stretches out into the surrounding landscape, keeping the sun off not only the foyer but also several acres of terraces, gardens and pools, and offering a seamless transition from city to park to foyer to auditorium. One can imagine an urban version of Glyndebourne, with the setting providing for picnics in the park before the performance.

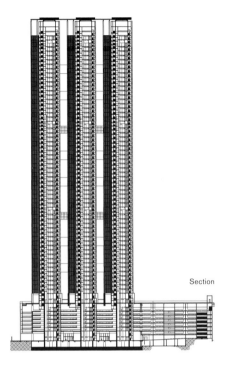

Section

THE MET
BANGKOK, THAILAND

**WITHDRAWN BY THE ARCHITECTS FROM THE
2010 RIBA LUBETKIN PRIZE SHORTLIST OWING
TO THE POLITICAL SITUATION**

WOHA WITH TANDEM ARCHITECTS 2001

CLIENT: PEBBLE BAY THAILAND
STRUCTURAL ENGINEER: WORLEY
SERVICES ENGINEER: EEC LINCOLNE SCOTT THAILAND
LANDSCAPE CONSULTANT: CICADA
CONTRACTOR: BOUYGUES THAI
CONTACT VALUE: $132,000,000
DATE OF OCCUPATION: DECEMBER 2009
GROSS INTERNAL AREA: 112,833,523 SQ. M
IMAGES: PATRICK BINGHAM-HALL

Unlike most towers in hot climates, which mimic the high-rise
solutions of cold climates, this sixty-six-storey residential building
works with the climate, capturing the stronger breezes and cleaner
air at such levels. Residents also enjoy improved security, more
privacy, less noise and dust, and great views. Yet they still get the
benefits of low-level living: gardens, shared open spaces and pools.

This green tower uses only minimal air conditioning. Green
creeper screens create living walls right up to the top floor to help
shade the occupants and cool the building through transpiration.
It takes clever architecture to pull all this off, and WOHA are indeed
intelligent architects. The Met shows that an alternative strategy to
the sleek, air-conditioned box can work in the tropics, and this has
implications everywhere.

SPANISH PAVILION, EXPO 2010 SHANGHAI
SHANGHAI, CHINA

MIRALLES TAGLIABUE EMBT

CLIENT: SOCIEDAD ESTATAL PARA EXPOSICIONES INTERNACIONALES
STRUCTURAL ENGINEER: ESTUDIO INGENIERIA
CONTRACTORS: INYPSA INFORMES Y PROYECTOS; CHINA CONSTRUCTION
     EIGHTH ENGINEERING DIVISION
GROSS INTERNAL AREA: 8500 SQ M
IMAGES: MIRALLES TAGLIABUE EMBT

The challenge for the architects of all national pavilions lies in creating a design that stands out in the crowd while providing a visitor experience that is more lasting than the instant hit of visual stimulation. EMBT's Spanish Pavilion at Expo 2010 Shanghai is one of a handful that achieved this tricky balancing act.

The vast structure is formed from a steel frame hung with 8500 panels of woven willow. The wicker walls are double curved in complex geometry to form a series of lofty halls, so the whole resembles the nest of a giant insect. EMBT has married the tradition of wicker-weaving (a craft common to Spain and China) with the modernity of computer form-making, producing both an immediate visual punch and, more satisfyingly, a longer-lasting effect of tactility and architectural form.

Section

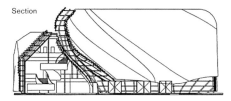

UNILEVER HEADQUARTERS
HAMBURG, GERMANY

BEHNISCH ARCHITEKTEN

CLIENT: RREEF INVESTMENT (PREVIOUSLY HOCHTIEF PROJEKTENTWICKLUNG)
LANDSCAPE ARCHITECTS: BEHNISCH ARCHITEKTEN WITH EMBT
STRUCTURAL ENGINEERS: WEBER POLL WITH PFEFFERKORN
SERVICES ENGINEER: HKP
CONTRACTOR: QUICKBORNER TEAM
CONTRACT VALUE: CONFIDENTIAL
DATE OF OCCUPATION: 2009
GROSS INTERNAL AREA: 35,235 SQ. M
IMAGES: ADAM MØRK

This headquarters building in Hamburg's new HafenCity represents a fine piece of city-making. Stefan Behnisch's buildings are always far greener than they look. The scheme uses solar-control glass to ensure that daylight is transmitted rather than heat, thus reducing the need for artificial lighting and cooling systems.

Movement through the atrium is remarkably barrier-free for a headquarters building; in fact, the public are encouraged to use its cross routes or be diverted by its coffee shops. Overall, the building combines structural ingenuity with exemplary environmental design, making for a holistic piece of architecture that is a pleasure to work in and somewhere for Hamburg citizens to enjoy. For the client, it makes a statement about a dynamic and forward-looking company.

Typical ground-floor plan

VILLALAGOS
PUNTA DEL ESTE, URUGUAY

KALLOS TURIN WITH ALVARO PEREZ

CLIENTS: OBSIDIAN CAPITAL WITH SIMON AND NATALIE FULLER
STRUCTURAL ENGINEER: ALFREDO FERNANDEZ
SERVICES ENGINEERS: ISTEC INGENIERA; JUAN SANGUINETTI
CONTRACTOR: BAUBETA
CONTRACT VALUE: $2,850,000
DATE OF OCCUPATION: APRIL 2009
GROSS INTERNAL AREA: 1357 SQ. M
IMAGES: DENNIS GILBERT – VIEW

The Villalagos project sets out to achieve minimalist luxury within
an outstanding natural landscape. The buildings – large, almost
quarry-like blocks of stone – are carved to enclose, contain or
define semi-outside spaces that bridge the interiors and the large
spaces beyond.

The architects set up a flowing rhythm of space, enclosure
and wall. Detailing is rigorous, consistent and fully resolved. The
landscape is nurtured to support wildlife and to lessen the impact
of the construction.

The buildings achieve that rarity: a perfect combination of
luxury, simplicity and elegance. The villas stand in splendid isolation
in the great landscape but at their core contain spaces that
encourage the theatre of family life.

THE RIBA MANSER MEDAL
IN ASSOCIATION WITH HSBC PRIVATE BANK

The objectives of the RIBA Manser Medal are to encourage innovation in house design, to show how social and technological ambitions can be met by intelligent design, and to produce exemplars to be taken up by the wider house-building industry. The prize is named after Michael Manser, former RIBA President, who is well known for his own steel-and-glass house designs.

Michael Manser had for a number of years chaired the National Homebuilder Design Awards, which were run by Mike Gazzard. Gazzard approached Tony Chapman, custodian of all the RIBA's awards, about how to mark Manser's contribution. It was agreed to create an award in his name for one-off houses, by way of balancing the Housing Design Awards, which are exclusively for housing schemes. The Manser Medal was presented as part of the National Homebuilder Design Awards for two years, before switching stables in 2003 to become part of the RIBA Awards. In 2006 the National Homebuilder Design Awards were bought by EMAP, long-term sponsors of the RIBA's awards programme. The award has since been presented at the RIBA Awards Dinner and latterly at the RIBA Stirling Prize Dinner, even twice being televised.

The RIBA Manser Medal was relaunched with HSBC Private Bank as the exclusive sponsor for 2010–11. Eligibility for the medal reverted to the traditional position of being open only to one-off houses. The prize money was doubled to £10,000, and a new trophy was commissioned from artist Petr Weigl, who also designed the plaque for the RIBA Lubetkin Prize. All the RIBA Award-winning houses in the United Kingdom were considered for this year's medal, and six were shortlisted. The winner was announced at an event held at the RIBA on 11 November 2010.

For previous winners of the medal, see p. 255.

WINNER

HUNSETT MILL
STALHAM, NORFOLK
ACME

SHORTLIST

BATEMAN'S ROW
LONDON EC2
THEIS + KHAN ARCHITECTS

FURZEY HALL FARM
GLOUCESTERSHIRE
WAUGH THISTLETON ARCHITECTS

LEAF HOUSE
LONDON NW3
JAMES GORST ARCHITECTS

MARTELLO TOWER Y
BAWDSEY, SUFFOLK
PIERCY CONNER ARCHITECTS
WITH BILLINGS JACKSON DESIGN

ZERO-CARBON HOUSE
TINDAL STREET, BIRMINGHAM
JOHN CHRISTOPHERS

JUDGES

MICHAEL MANSER, CBE
FORMER RIBA PRESIDENT

DEBORAH SAUNT
ARCHITECT, DSDHA

LUKE TOZER
ARCHITECT, PITMAN TOZER
ARCHITECTS

PETER MACKIE
PROPERTY VISION, A DIVISION
OF HSBC PRIVATE BANK

TONY CHAPMAN
RIBA HEAD OF AWARDS

HUNSETT MILL
STALHAM, NORFOLK

ACME

CLIENTS: CATRIONA AND JOHN DODSWORTH; JOANNA AND JON EMERY
STRUCTURAL ENGINEER: ADAMS KARA TAYLOR (GERRY O'BRIEN, GARY LYNCH)
SERVICES ENGINEER: HOARE LEA (PHIL GREW)
CONTRACTORS: WILLOW BUILDERS; EURBAN (TIMBER STRUCTURE); NUTTALL
    (FLOOD DEFENCE)
CONTRACT VALUE: £600,000
DATE OF COMPLETION: AUGUST 2009
GROSS INTERNAL AREA: 215 SQ. M
IMAGES: FRIEDRICH LUDEWIG (P. 74 BOTTOM); CRISTOBAL PALMA – VIEW (TOP;
    BOTTOM LEFT AND RIGHT; P. 74 TOP; P. 75 TOP)
LONGLISTED FOR THE RIBA STIRLING PRIZE AND SHORTLISTED FOR THE
    STEPHEN LAWRENCE PRIZE

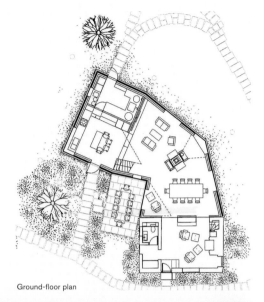

Ground-floor plan

Hunsett Mill is a very specific response to a very specific space: an arcadian setting on the Norfolk Broads. The windmill and its outbuildings appear on jigsaws, postcards and chocolate boxes as a famous view from narrowboats. The new building is conceived as a shadow sitting within the site lines of the retained cottage, so that the new building is invisible from the water.

The new building is clad in black charred timber so that it is truly a shadow, with flush glazing that adds to the sense of insubstantiality. The overall impact is very arresting – more akin to the response to a piece of art than an example of rural domestic architecture. As such, it is a brilliant and beautifully realized idea.

The drama of the architectural response seems entirely appropriate to this busy thoroughfare of the Norfolk Broads, where progress is necessarily slow and lingering.

The judges enjoyed the constant inventiveness of Acme's approach, which sought new materials and utilized intriguing structural forms to create interesting shapes, values and visual effects. The building is used as a weekend or holiday home by a number of families. This usage allows the interiors to continue the inventiveness and drama of the exterior forms without too many domestic constraints.

The roof forms are particularly enjoyable, creating a series of linked gables that are asymmetric but rhythmic. Further changes of angle are added to make a series of interesting spaces, with the first-floor walkway to the bedrooms being particularly special. The whole is consistently detailed and well crafted, with interesting use of off-site construction.

Overall, the restoration of the cottage and the new building, which are linked internally, are an exciting and intellectually stimulating response to the strange rural setting. The cultured clients have given free rein to the innovation of their chosen architect, Acme, and engineers Adams Kara Taylor.

Hunsett Mill proves that good architecture can be delivered on a budget and that it can be achieved in the most restrictive of situations; as a planning authority, Norfolk is not renowned for risk-taking. The resulting project balances value and quality, and is one to which many people could aspire.

BATEMAN'S ROW
LONDON EC2

THEIS + KHAN ARCHITECTS

CLIENTS: SORAYA KHAN AND PATRICK THEIS

This is an economically sustainable development by the architect-clients for a mix of uses, including their home and studio, a gallery and three apartments. In section, the scheme skilfully adjusts the floor heights, creating taller spaces for the gallery, the studio and the principal living space.

This is a great city-making building, with the kind of scale and mix that is both ordinary and relevant; but, because it is executed with extraordinary care and judgement, it is the sort of building of which London needs a lot more.

For the full citation, see pp. 30–33.

FURZEY HALL FARM
GLOUCESTERSHIRE

WAUGH THISTLETON ARCHITECTS

CLIENT: PRIVATE

A Victorian Cotswold-stone farm cottage and barn have been restored and linked by an elegant new L-shaped single-storey timber-and-glass building accommodating an open-plan kitchen/dining area that opens on to a decked terrace and a reed-bed swimming pool.

The thick rubblework exterior walls are now absorbed into the interior, providing a delightful contrast to the smooth, minimal finishes of the new building. Ground-source heat pumps supply heating and hot water.

For the full citation, see p. 146.

LEAF HOUSE
LONDON NW3

JAMES GORST ARCHITECTS

CLIENT: PRIVATE

This is a thoughtful contemporary interpretation of a traditional large London town house. There is one study in the pavilion on the roof and another in the basement, lit by a glass pavement-light.

This is a large house, but it is extremely well judged. Acoustic separation of spaces was key to the brief, and there are many neat details, such as doors that can close off otherwise open-plan arrangements into separate spaces. Overall simplicity is overlaid with richness of detail.

For the full citation, see p. 170.

MARTELLO TOWER Y
BAWDSEY, SUFFOLK

PIERCY CONNER ARCHITECTS
WITH BILLINGS JACKSON DESIGN

CLIENTS: DUNCAN AND KRISTIN JACKSON

The Martello Tower presents the housing architect with manifold challenges. From the bureaucratic point of view, one has to consider how to deal with a scheduled ancient monument in an Area of Outstanding Natural Beauty. Then there is the problem of how to introduce services into a structure with 4-metre-thick walls elegantly and unobtrusively; and finally, how to design in a way that sees the shape as an advantage, not a hindrance, to creativity. The architects' sensitive response is typified by the beauty of the exposed domed brickwork and the indoor–outdoor roof terrace.

For the full citation, see p. 140.

ZERO-CARBON HOUSE
TINDAL STREET, BIRMINGHAM

JOHN CHRISTOPHERS

CLIENTS: JO HINDLEY AND JOHN CHRISTOPHERS

Past winner of the RIBA Sustainability Award John Christophers has made a family home of rare quality using low-energy materials and environmental systems. It is the first UK retrofit house to achieve zero carbon standards as defined in the Code for Sustainable Homes Level 6.

Externally, the house has a completely different character from the rest of the terrace, but really adds to the urban streetscape. It is full of quirky, delightful and well-considered details, and is a robust and thoughtful design of exceptional quality.

For the full citation, see p. 133.

THE RIBA
SPECIAL AWARDS

The RIBA Special Awards are chosen from RIBA
Award-winners and are judged by panels that
include specialist judges in the various fields,
who pay further visits to the shortlisted buildings.
The shortlists for the five awards reflect the
diversity of architecture and reward the wide
variety of specialist skills involved in delivering
good buildings.

THE CROWN ESTATE CONSERVATION AWARD

THE RIBA CLIENT OF THE YEAR
SUPPORTED BY THE BLOXHAM CHARITABLE TRUST

THE RIBA CABE PUBLIC SPACE AWARD

THE RIBA SORRELL FOUNDATION SCHOOLS AWARDS

THE STEPHEN LAWRENCE PRIZE
SUPPORTED BY THE MARCO GOLDSCHMIED FOUNDATION

THE CROWN ESTATE CONSERVATION AWARD

The Crown Estate Conservation Award is made to the architect of the work that best demonstrates the successful restoration and/or adaptation of an architecturally significant building. It carries a prize of £5000.

The Crown Estate manages a large and uniquely diverse portfolio of land and buildings across the United Kingdom. One of its primary concerns is to demonstrate that conservation is not a dry, academic discipline but a practical art, making yesterday's buildings work for people today.

For previous winners of the award, see p. 255.

WINNER

NEUES MUSEUM
MUSEUMINSEL, BERLIN, GERMANY
DAVID CHIPPERFIELD ARCHITECTS
IN COLLABORATION WITH
JULIAN HARRAP

SHORTLIST

ALDEBURGH MUSIC CREATIVE
CAMPUS
SNAPE MALTINGS, SUFFOLK
HAWORTH TOMPKINS

CORPUS CHRISTI COLLEGE
AUDITORIUM
MERTON STREET, OXFORD
RICK MATHER ARCHITECTS

THE MONUMENT
LONDON EC3
JULIAN HARRAP ARCHITECTS

NORWICH CATHEDRAL HOSTRY
THE CLOSE, NORWICH
HOPKINS ARCHITECTS WITH
HENRY FREELAND, ARCHITECT
TO NORWICH CATHEDRAL

JUDGES

RICHARD GRIFFITHS
CONSERVATION ARCHITECT,
RICHARD GRIFFITHS ARCHITECTS

PAUL VELLUET
CONSERVATION ARCHITECT, HOK

ROGER BRIGHT
CHIEF EXECUTIVE, THE CROWN
ESTATE

TONY CHAPMAN
RIBA HEAD OF AWARDS

NEUES MUSEUM
MUSEUMINSEL, BERLIN, GERMANY

DAVID CHIPPERFIELD ARCHITECTS IN COLLABORATION WITH JULIAN HARRAP

CLIENT: STIFTUNG PREUSSISCHER KULTURBESITZ
STRUCTURAL ENGINEER: INGENIEURGRUPPE BAUEN
SERVICES ENGINEER: JMP
QUANTITY SURVEYOR: NANNA FÜTTERER FOR DAVID CHIPPERFIELD
    ARCHITECTS
CONTRACTOR: BUNDESAMT FÜR BAUWESEN UND RAUMORDNUNG
CONTRACT VALUE: €200,000,000
DATE OF OCCUPATION: OCTOBER 2009
GROSS INTERNAL AREA: 20,500 SQ. M
IMAGES: JÖRG VON BRUCHHAUSEN (BOTTOM); CHRISTIAN RICHTERS – VIEW
    (TOP; P. 82 BOTTOM; P. 83); UTE ZSCHARNT (P. 82 TOP)
SHORTLISTED FOR THE RIBA STIRLING PRIZE

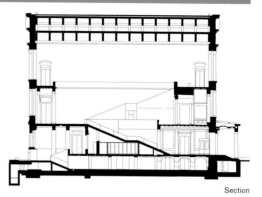

Section

Designed by Friedrich August Stüler and built between 1841 and 1859, the Neues Museum is located on Museum Island on the River Spree in the historic, cultural heart of Berlin, and is an integral part of a unique group of nineteenth-century museum and gallery buildings, including Karl Friedrich Schinkel's memorable Altes Museum of 1830. The Neues Museum housed an unrivalled collection of antiquities, among them a remarkable collection of ancient Egyptian art, but suffered major damage in the last part of the Second World War, and remained in a substantially ruined state until recent times.

The architects have placed emphasis on revealing and celebrating the surviving, massive brick structure of the original building; on repairing and reconstructing, where necessary with exemplary care, the impressive vaulted, hollow, clay-pot ceilings throughout the building; on repairing surviving sections of the unusual roof structures and introducing new, boldly scaled roof carpentry; and on recovering and retrieving the surviving parts of the outstanding original scheme of internal painted decoration within the galleries and circulation spaces. Importantly, the work

has also included the reconstruction of the very fine colonnade running along the south and east elevations of the museum and extending around the newly landscaped space that links together the other cultural buildings, reusing the damaged columns from the original building.

The architects have shown discernment in judging and determining the balance between works of repair and reinstatement and the introduction of distinct new work. Most impressive are the design and detailing of the significant new work within the two glazed courtyards (the Egyptian Courtyard and the Greek Courtyard) and in the heroically scaled Staircase Hall at the heart of the museum. Such works have created highly animated and attractive spaces in which visitors can orientate themselves with ease within the vast building.

An archaeological approach to the treatment of the surviving fabric has been tempered by an artistic approach to the integration of the reconstructed and surviving parts in order to create an aesthetic whole. The result is an exemplary reworking of a fine old building.

THE RIBA
CLIENT OF THE YEAR
SUPPORTED BY THE BLOXHAM CHARITABLE TRUST

The RIBA Client of the Year was established in 1998 to acknowledge the significant role played by the client in the creation of fine architecture. The RIBA's partner for many years was Arts Council England. The fifth winner, in 2002, was Urban Splash, for 'its commitment both to design and quality and the regeneration of Manchester and Liverpool'. Urban Splash's co-founder Tom Bloxham is supporting the award in 2010 through the Bloxham Charitable Trust.

In order to be considered for the award, it is necessary for the client to have commissioned an RIBA Award-winning building in the year in question. Traditionally, the award is presented to a client that has a track record of exemplary commissioning, rather than a client that has commissioned a one-off building. An exception was made in 2009, when the Awards Group felt that the number of exceptional 'one-off' and 'serial' clients justified the award being given to six joint winners.

For previous winners of the award, see p. 256.

WINNER

HAMMERSON

SHORTLIST

ALDEBURGH MUSIC

NHS GREATER GLASGOW AND CLYDE

THE ROYAL PARKS

VICTORIA AND ALBERT MUSEUM

JUDGES

Tom Bloxham and members of the RIBA Awards Group following visits to the relevant schemes and meetings with the nominated clients

HAMMERSON for 60 Threadneedle Street by Eric Parry
Architects (below) and Twenty Bishops Square/St Botolph's Hall
by Matthew Lloyd Architects, both in London. In 2009 Hammerson
also commissioned two RIBA Award-winning buildings: the House
of Fraser store at Cabot Circus, Bristol, by Stanton Williams;
and the John Lewis store and cineplex, Leicester, by Foreign
Office Architects.

Hammerson is the 2010 Client of the Year for its commitment
to supporting fine architecture. Working with a mix of established
and younger architects, it has produced commercial architecture of
rare quality. Having accepted the architects' arguments that high-
quality design and materials equal good value, it refrained from any
serious cost-cutting. The result is Foreign Office's striking 'net
curtain'-patterned glazing at Leicester, the artist Susanna Heron's
etched-glass windows in Stanton Williams's Bristol store and
the beautifully detailed oriel-window shopfronts in Parry's
Threadneedle Street.

The client takes obvious pride in all these achievements, and
the work represents a metamorphosis of desire and ambition at
Hammerson that has cemented a relationship with and a respect
for architecture.

For the full project citations, see pp. 161 and 182.

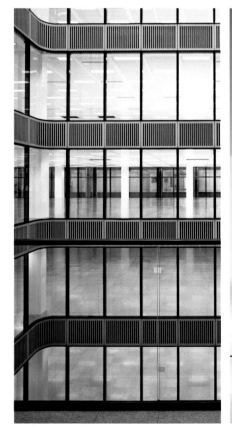

ALDEBURGH MUSIC for the conversion and extension of Snape Maltings for rehearsal rooms and studios by Haworth Tompkins. Aldeburgh Music's political skill, technical experience and attention to detail, underpinned by an articulate artistic vision of the new facilities, allowed the architect to realize this project with confidence. Aldeburgh has previously commissioned Purcell Miller Tritton and Penoyre & Prasad to add to Arup's fine work.

For the full project citation, see p. 137.

NHS GREATER GLASGOW AND CLYDE for New Stobhill Hospital, Glasgow, by Reiach and Hall Architects. This commission represents a major step forward in the sustainable provision of modern health care; it reduces the cost of care and increases its effectiveness. Project director Alex McIntyre proved capable of taking significant decisions and appointed a talented project sponsor, Margaret Campbell, facilitating a level of conversation rarely seen in large health-care projects.

For the full project citation, see p. 106.

THE ROYAL PARKS for the 7 July Memorial, Hyde Park, by
Carmody Groarke, and for a series of earlier commissions in
London's Royal Parks, including the Diana, Princess of Wales
Memorial Fountain in Hyde Park by Gustafson Porter; the annual
temporary Serpentine Gallery Pavilions in Kensington Gardens;
and David Morley Architects' Hub sports pavilion and the new
Open Air Theatre by Haworth Tompkins, both in Regent's Park.
For the 7 July Memorial the client Colin Buttery, Director of Parks,
formed a project board that was prepared to take on a newly
established practice and to work unsentimentally, impartially and
collaboratively to produce a fitting memorial for the families of the
victims and for London as a whole.

For the full project citation, see p. 160.

VICTORIA AND ALBERT MUSEUM for the Medieval &
Renaissance Galleries by MUMA with Julian Harrap Architects
(right), and the Sackler Centre for Arts Education by Softroom.
These schemes completed phase one of the £120 million
FuturePlan, which began with the British Galleries project.
Historically, the museum has had the conviction to commission
young designers, a tradition that dates back to the young William
Morris, who designed the Morris Room in 1866. The appointment
of MUMA and Softroom was in the same spirit, and demonstrates
the V&A's belief in design and its commitment to support the use
of innovative technologies and craftsmanship.

For the full project citations, see pp. 173 and 181.

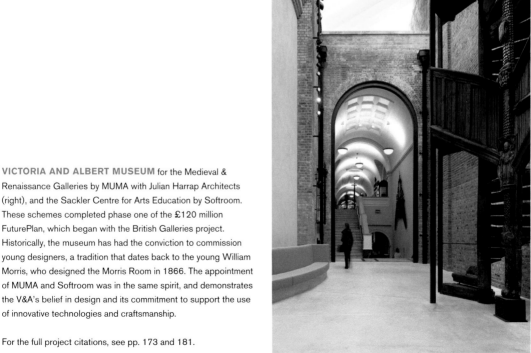

THE RIBA CABE
PUBLIC SPACE AWARD

The £5000 RIBA CABE Public Space Award is sponsored by the Commission for Architecture and the Built Environment (CABE). The prize is presented to the architect and landscape architect of the best RIBA Award-winning public space in the United Kingdom, and recognizes the valuable contribution that a well-designed public realm makes to the quality of the built environment and of our daily lives.

For previous winners of the award, see p. 256.

WINNER

PIER HEAD AND CANAL LINK
GEORGES PARADE, LIVERPOOL
AECOM DESIGN + PLANNING

SHORTLIST

7 JULY MEMORIAL
HYDE PARK, LONDON W1
CARMODY GROARKE WITH
LANDSCAPE ARCHITECT
COLVIN & MOGGRIDGE

REGENT'S PLACE PAVILION
LONDON NW1
CARMODY GROARKE

JUDGES

SARAH GAVENTA
DIRECTOR, CABE SPACE

RENATO BENEDETTI
ARCHITECT, MCDOWELL +
BENEDETTI ARCHITECTS

TONY CHAPMAN
RIBA HEAD OF AWARDS

PIER HEAD AND CANAL LINK
GEORGES PARADE, LIVERPOOL

AECOM DESIGN + PLANNING

CLIENTS: LIVERPOOL CITY COUNCIL; BRITISH WATERWAYS
STRUCTURAL ENGINEER: ARUP
SERVICES ENGINEER: 2020 LIVERPOOL
CONTRACTOR: BALFOUR BEATTY CIVIL ENGINEERING
CONTRACT VALUE: £22,000,000
DATE OF COMPLETION: JUNE 2009
GROSS AREA: 25,000 SQ. M
IMAGES: LEE CARUS (TOP); ANT CLAUSEN (P. 90 TOP; P. 91 BOTTOM); ALAN
        COOKSON (P. 91 TOP); DARREN JOHNSTON (BOTTOM; P. 90 BOTTOM)

Pier Head Liverpool creates an exceptional new waterfront for the city. The scheme is as graceful as its three famous neighbours and complements them in an elegant and subtle manner.

This is an ambitious project, part of an EDAW (now AECOM) masterplan for the regeneration of the Liverpool Maritime Mercantile City World Heritage Site, which is extended to include the new Museum of Liverpool, a mixed-use development of homes, shops and offices, and a remodelled Mersey Ferry Terminal. Key to the success of the project is, however, the engineering of a new stretch of the Leeds and Liverpool Canal, linking it to the basins of the old Kings Dock and bringing tourist boats down to the Pier Head. With the adjacent cruise-liner terminal and the nearby Liverpool One

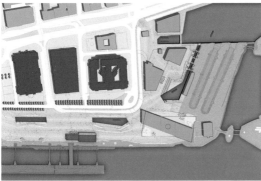

Site plan

development, the new Pier Head completes the work begun by James Stirling's restored Albert Dock and Tate Gallery to draw the city's centre of gravity back to the river.

The new public space has managed to retain its simple and strong design quality through a long and complex process. Gentle and seamless changes in levels create a topography that is fluid, easy to read and usable for all. Places of refuge from the elements, as well as vantage points, are clever and well integrated, allowing the space to function equally well as a venue for major events and as a place for quiet contemplation. The craftsmanship, quality and attention to detail are exemplary and result in a space that aims to encourage people to linger and enjoy – and they do.

The materials used throughout are robust and designed for long life. Solid stone was used for the seats instead of the planned stone-clad concrete, and the blocks were cut using computer-controlled machines. The space is well but atmospherically lit by night and surveilled by cameras and patrols. As a result, it is safe and there has been virtually no vandalism.

This is place-making at its best, creating a space that is well used by the public and well managed by the council. It is an obvious labour of love for all involved, a truly impressive achievement and in the judges' opinion the true fourth grace.

THE RIBA
SORRELL FOUNDATION
SCHOOLS AWARDS

The RIBA Sorrell Foundation Schools Award is
presented to the architect of the best RIBA
Award-winning school – primary or secondary –
with the aim of raising the standards of design in
all new school building. The Sorrell Foundation
sets out to inspire creativity in young people and
to improve quality of life through good design,
connecting such public sectors as education
and health with the elite of the United Kingdom's
design community.

For previous winners of the award, see p. 256.

WINNER

ST LUKE'S CHURCH OF ENGLAND
AIDED PRIMARY SCHOOL
PARK STREET SOUTH,
WOLVERHAMPTON
ARCHITYPE

SHORTLIST

CHRIST'S COLLEGE
LARCH AVENUE, GUILDFORD
DSDHA

CLAPHAM MANOR PRIMARY SCHOOL
LONDON SW4
DRMM

LOWTHER CHILDREN'S CENTRE
STILLINGFLEET ROAD, LONDON SW13
PATEL TAYLOR

REDNOCK SCHOOL
KINGSHILL ROAD, DURSLEY,
GLOUCESTERSHIRE
CUBE DESIGN

JUDGES

LADY FRANCES SORRELL
CO-FOUNDER OF THE SORRELL
FOUNDATION

IAN GOODFELLOW
ARCHITECT, PENOYRE & PRASAD

MUKUND PATEL
BUSINESS DEVELOPMENT
DIRECTOR, SAMMON GROUP;
FORMER DIRECTOR OF BUILDING
SCHOOLS FOR THE FUTURE

ST LUKE'S CHURCH OF ENGLAND AIDED PRIMARY SCHOOL
PARK STREET SOUTH, WOLVERHAMPTON

ARCHITYPE

CLIENTS: WOLVERHAMPTON CITY COUNCIL; DIOCESE OF LICHFIELD
LANDSCAPE DESIGNER: COE DESIGN
STRUCTURAL ENGINEER: PRICE & MYERS
SERVICES ENGINEER: E3 CONSULTING ENGINEERS
CONTRACTOR: THOMAS VALE CONSTRUCTION
CONTRACT VALUE: £5,991,771
DATE OF COMPLETION: JUNE 2009
GROSS INTERNAL AREA: 2911 SQ. M
IMAGES: LEIGH SIMPSON

St Luke's, the first primary school in Britain to receive a BREEAM 'Excellent' rating, is designed to achieve a transformational approach to education, within a standard budget.

Anyone involved in building a new primary school – be they head teachers and staff, pupils and parents or architects and councillors – should see this school before doing anything else. It is a wonderful exemplar of new ways of teaching, learning and approaching integrated sustainability, resulting from great teamwork among the pupils, the staff and the design team. In the humanist tradition, Architype has created a calm, welcoming yet uplifting environment in which to learn and teach, and one that is very well

Section

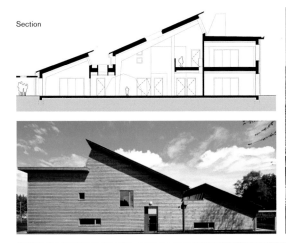

considered, down to the smallest detail, for the people it serves. The landscaping by Coe Design complements the architecture and helps to remove one from the gritty inner-city site, providing a semi-rural experience for all.

With its high levels of daylighting and controlled solar gain, this is an exceptional building, and it is helping to transform a deprived area. Its execution has been rigorous; its detailing is immaculate. There are timber shingles on the roof, beautiful timber ceilings, and coloured glazing to reference the eponymous church.

The school has no corridors where trouble can start. Instead, two light, airy hubs provide naturally ventilated classrooms grouped around social spaces. The architecture makes for a genuine sense of community and allows children of different ages to interact in a way that simply does not happen in most schools today. The plan also works well for out-of-hours activities, with security discreetly and effectively accommodated. Large sliding glass screens extend classrooms outside under generous canopies, which also provide sun-screening and shelter from the rain.

The architect describes its approach as 'eco-minimalism', which provides good levels of daylight and allows all spaces to be naturally ventilated. All the structural timber is prefabricated, and the buildings are insulated with recycled newspapers. Windows are triple-glazed throughout. The children can monitor their building's energy performance thanks to a link between their computers and the building-management system.

Teachers testify that it is a pleasure to teach in the school, and pupils that there are worse places in which to learn.

THE STEPHEN LAWRENCE PRIZE
SUPPORTED BY THE MARCO GOLDSCHMIED FOUNDATION

The Stephen Lawrence Prize is supported by the Marco Goldschmied Foundation. The prize commemorates the teenager who was just setting out on the road to becoming an architect when he was murdered in 1993. It rewards the best examples of projects with a construction budget of less than £1,000,000. In addition to the £5000 prize money, Marco Goldschmied donates £10,000 to fund the Stephen Lawrence Scholarship at the Architectural Association in London.

The Stephen Lawrence Prize was established in 1998 to draw attention to the Stephen Lawrence Trust, which assists young black students in studying architecture, and to reward the creativity required for smaller projects with low budgets.

For previous winners of the award, see p. 257.

WINNER

ARTISTS' HOUSE
LONDON W8
GUMUCHDJIAN ARCHITECTS

SHORTLIST

1–5 BATEMAN MEWS
LONDON SW4
ANNE THORNE ARCHITECTS
PARTNERSHIP

7 JULY MEMORIAL
HYDE PARK, LONDON W1
CARMODY GROARKE

BUS DRIVER FACILITY
CHEQUERS LANE, DAGENHAM
JULIAN COWIE ARCHITECTS

HUNSETT MILL
STALHAM, NORFOLK
ACME

MARTELLO TOWER Y
BAWDSEY, SUFFOLK
PIERCY CONNER ARCHITECTS WITH
BILLINGS JACKSON DESIGN

JUDGES

MARCO GOLDSCHMIED
ARCHITECT

PANKAJ PATEL
ARCHITECT, PATEL TAYLOR

DOREEN LAWRENCE, OBE

TONY CHAPMAN
RIBA HEAD OF AWARDS

ARTISTS' HOUSE
LONDON W8

GUMUCHDJIAN ARCHITECTS

CLIENTS: VALENTINE AND REGIS FRANC
LANDSCAPE ARCHITECT: TODD LONGSTAFFE-GOWAN
STRUCTURAL ENGINEER: CONISBEE
CONTRACTOR: ROBIN ELLIS PROJECTS
CONTRACT VALUE: £926,000
DATE OF COMPLETION: JANUARY 2008
GROSS INTERNAL AREA: 400 SQ. M
IMAGES: RICHARD DAVIES (P. 98); PHILIP GUMUCHDJIAN (LEFT; RIGHT, TOP AND
    BOTTOM; P. 99)

During the Second World War a bomb that fell on a Kensington
side street demolished the original speculative housing built for the
Great Exhibition in the mid-nineteenth century, opening up a site for
a low-budget mid-twentieth-century replacement terrace, one of
which has now been transformed into a bespoke family home for an
artist/writer/designer couple who work from home. The brief was to
create a flexible, multifunctional, spatially diverse house. This has
been achieved with an understated confidence. Like a minimalist
Sir John Soane's Museum, the complete reworking gives few
external clues to the sophisticated and quirky interior.

The beautifully detailed floating stair provides the vertical focus
of the design, from which the spaces open up. The house is full of

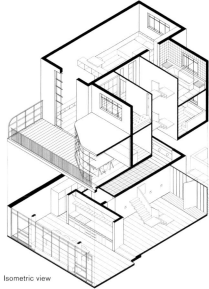

Isometric view

surprises and light. Another fine example is the discrete curved office, which extends out from an original bedroom to occupy a section of the first-floor terrace. This terrace is the roof of a doubled-in-size lower-ground-floor kitchen, which was created by building a concrete 'table' out into the garden. None of the additions cries out; rather, they give the interior extra shots of brilliant light. The spaces are varied and distinct, yet a great sense of fluidity, illumination and visual connection is achieved.

A dramatic exotic garden has been created that complements the house perfectly, the French/Mediterranean planting clearly resonating with its French owners. The gigantic palm trees were left – at the architect's insistence – where the nursery dumped them on delivery, just outside the full-height kitchen windows, providing shade. The garden is then theatrically pulled into the kitchen by means of reflections in a linear angled mirror above the work surface. The detailing and the spare use of quality materials successfully reference Bauhaus while being clearly grounded in the twenty-first century. The scheme is an exemplar of what can be achieved when an enlightened client collaborates with an inventive architect.

From the clever opening up of the rear garden to the sweeping, top-lit three-storey staircase, the overall effect is to transform a utilitarian box into a glorious continuum of spaces, flowing and interconnecting in unexpected ways, with every corner bringing an unexpected delight.

THE RIBA AWARDS

The RIBA Awards were established in 1966. RIBA members are invited to enter projects for all the RIBA building awards in the first two months of the year. Entries are first visited by a local architect to see if they merit a visit from a full regional jury of three, consisting of an architect chair from outside the region, one from that region and a 'lay' juror, such as an engineer, client, artist or journalist. The chairs of the regional juries report to the Awards Group (the scheme's advisory panel), which has the right to query if a scheme not given an award was, in its view, worthy of one. In this case, the jury chair may, in consultation with the other members of his or her jury, agree to an award. The Awards Group has no right to overturn an award. These awards are presented in the RIBA regions.

JUDGES

THE REGIONAL JUDGES ARE LISTED IN THE FOLLOWING ORDER: CHAIR, REGIONAL REPRESENTATIVE AND LAY ASSESSOR

SCOTLAND
SIMON CONDER
DAVID DUNBAR
ANDY MACMILLAN

NORTHERN IRELAND
ANDY GROARKE
CLYDE MARKWELL
MORAG MYERSCOUGH

NORTH-EAST
JAMES SOANE
DOLAN CONWAY
PETER MILLICAN

NORTH-WEST
SAM JACOB
MATT BROOK
VICTORIA JESSEN-PIKE

YORKSHIRE
ROGER STEPHENSON
JOHN ORRELL
EMMA ENGLAND

WALES
MARTIN KNIGHT
BARRIE WILLIAMS
COLIN HAYWARD

WEST MIDLANDS
CHRISTOPHER WILLIAMSON
ROBERT TOLLEY
CATHERINE INCE

EAST MIDLANDS
MEREDITH BOWLES
KANTI CHHAPI
MALCOLM READING

EAST
RUSSELL BROWN
MICHAEL INNES
DAISY FROUD

SOUTH-WEST
PETER BARBER
SIMON BEESON
CHRISTINA SMITH

WESSEX
PETER BARBER
SIMON BEESON
CHRISTINA SMITH

SOUTH
JOHN PARDEY
PHILIP WADDY
LIZ PEACE

SOUTH-EAST
JOHN LYALL
GRAHAM WHITEHOUSE
ANDREW SEDGEWICK

LONDON EAST
ALEX DE RIJKE
DOMINIC PAPA
LUCY BULLIVANT

LONDON NORTH
RICHARD LAVINGTON
DAVID MIKHAIL
CRISPIN KELLY

LONDON SOUTH
GRAHAM HAWORTH
AMIN TAHA
SARAH ICHIOKA

LONDON WEST
JULIA BARFIELD
LUKE TOZER
GILLIAN DARLEY

EUROPEAN UNION
PAUL MONAGHAN (CHAIR)
BOB ALLIES
GIANNI BOTSFORD
ALISON BROOKS
TONY CHAPMAN
PETER CLEGG
TOM DYCKHOFF
PAUL FINCH
MURRAY FRASER
RICHARD GRIFFITHS
PHILIP GUMUCHDJIAN
FARSHID MOUSSAVI
DEBORAH SAUNT
BILL TAYLOR
CINDY WALTERS

ABERDEEN REGIONAL SPORTS FACILITY
LINKSFIELD ROAD, ABERDEEN

REIACH AND HALL ARCHITECTS

CLIENTS: ABERDEEN CITY COUNCIL; UNIVERSITY OF ABERDEEN;
    SPORTSCOTLAND
STRUCTURAL ENGINEER: SKM ANTHONY HUNT
SERVICES ENGINEERS: K.J. TAIT ENGINEERS; WALLACE WHITTLE
CONTRACTOR: BARR CONSTRUCTION
CONTRACT VALUE: £24,000,000
DATE OF COMPLETION: AUGUST 2009
GROSS INTERNAL AREA: 17,650 SQ. M
IMAGES: IOANA MARINESCU

This is a beautifully conceived and executed new sports resource for this part of Scotland, and is clearly very popular with both its staff and its users, a mixture of elite sportsmen and women as well as members of the wider community.

The architect has created a big building that has a lightness of touch so that it does not overwhelm its suburban surroundings. The use of subtly coloured polycarbonate sheeting, in a variety of different tones, allows the building to take on an ethereal quality as it merges with the skyscape above.

Internally, the building is light and airy. The plan is admirably simple, arranged around a central 4-metre-wide 'street' that encourages visual interaction between the different sports areas.

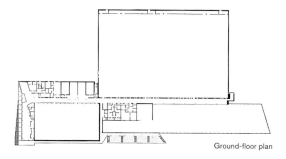

Ground-floor plan

BALNEARN BOATHOUSE
FEARNAN, LOCH TAYSIDE

MCKENZIE STRICKLAND ASSOCIATES

CLIENT: PRIVATE
STRUCTURAL ENGINEER: JOHN ADDISON
CONTRACTOR: BLAIRISH DEVELOPMENTS
CONTRACT VALUE: CONFIDENTIAL
DATE OF COMPLETION: FEBRUARY 2008
GROSS INTERNAL AREA: 36 SQ. M
IMAGE: KEITH HUNTER – ARCAID

A magical and expressive little building set on a stunning site on the banks of Loch Tay, Balnearn Boathouse consists of two strongly contrasting elements: at water level a cave-like boathouse has been formed using blocks of local stone, and on this base sits a lightweight timber-and-steel structure with a large viewing deck. This upper structure, which is articulated with a dramatic cantilevered 'wing' roof, contains a living room that, thanks to the inclusion of a bathroom and mini kitchen, also doubles as a visitor's suite.

Well put together, the upper structure incorporates sliding folding glazed doors to allow the room to open out fully to the views, and sliding timber security shutters.

HOTEL MISSONI
GEORGE IV BRIDGE, EDINBURGH

ALLAN MURRAY ARCHITECTS

CLIENT: THE MOUND PROPERTY COMPANY
STRUCTURAL ENGINEER: SKM ANTHONY HUNT
SERVICES ENGINEER: RPS GREGORY
CONTRACTOR: SIR ROBERT MCALPINE
CONTRACT VALUE: £27,000,000
DATE OF COMPLETION: JUNE 2009
GROSS INTERNAL AREA: 11,989 SQ. M
IMAGES: KEITH HUNTER – ARCAID (TOP); GARETH PUGH (BOTTOM)

Hotel Missoni sits at a pivotal location on the cross axis of
Edinburgh's Old Town. At ground-floor level, restaurants and a
bank ensure that this new structure is very much part of the public
life of the city. The design philosophy embraces 'unity through
diversity', and this has created a strong identity for the new building
that responds to three radically different contexts: the medieval
Lawnmarket; the nineteenth-century George IV Bridge; and
bohemian Victoria Street.

A new loggia addresses each separate streetscape. The scale
of the building is mitigated by the contextual nature of each
elevation on its three separate streetscape frontages. This major
new structure on a crucial urban site reinterprets a lost Edinburgh
tradition of hard-won public spaces.

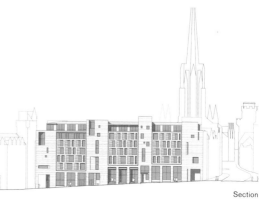

Section

103

HOUSE ON THE HILL
ABERDEENSHIRE

PATERSON ARCHITECTS

CLIENT: MAB LIMITED
STRUCTURAL ENGINEER: DAVID NARRO ASSOCIATES
ENVIRONMENTAL CONSULTANT: IRONSIDE FARRAR
CONTRACTOR: PERT BRUCE CONSTRUCTION
CONTRACT VALUE: £353,000
DATE OF COMPLETION: SEPTEMBER 2009
GROSS INTERNAL AREA: 260 SQ. M
IMAGES: KEITH HUNTER – ARCAID

Conventional planning wisdom has it that a residential extension should be smaller than, and subservient to, the original house. This entrancing and skilful extension of an existing croft is three times the size of the original and is certainly not subservient. Yet the strong contrast between new and old, and the linear hallway used to form a visual break between the two volumes, create a convincing and honest whole. It is a credit to the local planners, who rejected both 'reproduction' and total newbuild.

Internally, changes in level have been used to create a hierarchy of carefully considered spaces that add up to a warm and well-loved family home. The glazing has been placed with precision to capture the multiple views and flood the interior with light.

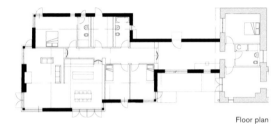

Floor plan

INFIRMARY STREET BATHS
INFIRMARY STREET, EDINBURGH

MALCOLM FRASER ARCHITECTS

CLIENT: DOVECOT PROPERTIES
STRUCTURAL ENGINEER: ELLIOTT & COMPANY
SERVICES ENGINEER: THE KEENAN CONSULTANCY
CONTRACTOR: REYWOOD CONSTRUCTION
CONTRACT VALUE: CONFIDENTIAL
DATE OF COMPLETION: AUGUST 2008
GROSS INTERNAL AREA: 4200 SQ. M
IMAGES: MALCOLM FRASER ARCHITECTS

This restoration and conversion of a redundant swimming-pool complex are an exemplar of how to reuse sound old buildings to produce a variety of new, viable and creative uses. Particularly impressive is the way in which the scheme includes flats and offices to help to fund the overall development of cultural facilities. Given the relative complexity of the site and the variety of functions that have been accommodated, the internal layout of the tapestry studio and gallery spaces is admirably simple and flexible.

The standard of construction and detailing is high, and there is a clear definition between new and old. This is a well-conceived project, and a great asset for both the tapestry-weaving and the local communities.

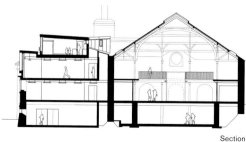

Section

NEW STOBHILL HOSPITAL
BALORNOCK ROAD, GLASGOW

REIACH AND HALL ARCHITECTS

CLIENT: NHS GREATER GLASGOW AND CLYDE
STRUCTURAL ENGINEER: SKM
SERVICES ENGINEER: DSSR
CONTRACTOR: BALFOUR BEATTY CONSTRUCTION
CONTRACT VALUE: £65,000,000
DATE OF COMPLETION: MARCH 2009
GROSS INTERNAL AREA: 28,000 SQ. M
IMAGES: ANDY MCGREGOR (TOP); MICHAEL WOLCHOVER (BOTTOM)
LONGLISTED FOR THE RIBA STIRLING PRIZE
NHS GREATER GLASGOW AND CLYDE WAS SHORTLISTED FOR THE RIBA CLIENT
    OF THE YEAR

The hospital is located in an area with challenging social and health problems, and serves more than 2000 patients a day. Externally, the building is modest but well considered; the real joy lies inside.

A linear atrium space divides treatment functions from consulting. This simple diagram, expressed in both plan and section, makes the building particularly easy to navigate. The design has not stopped at the level of the layout drawing, but has been effectively carried through to all aspects of the building, especially the waiting areas, which are enlivened by a series of planted courtyards and art installations. The overall spirit of the building is welcoming, warm and calm, which is largely down to the brilliant use of natural light.

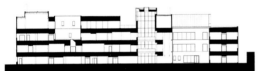

Section

SMALL ANIMAL HOSPITAL
BEARSDEN ROAD, GLASGOW

ARCHIAL ARCHITECTS

CLIENT: UNIVERSITY OF GLASGOW
LANDSCAPE ARCHITECT: CITY DESIGN CO-OPERATIVE
STRUCTURAL ENGINEER: BEATTIE WATKINSON PARTNERS
SERVICES ENGINEER: HULLEY & KIRKWOOD
CONTRACTOR: GRAHAM CONSTRUCTION
CONTRACT VALUE: £10,500,000
DATE OF COMPLETION: MAY 2009
GROSS INTERNAL AREA: 4502 SQ. M
IMAGES: ANDREW LEE

Located at the entrance to the grounds of Garscube Estate, the new Small Animal Hospital, which won the Royal Incorporation of Architects in Scotland's Andrew Doolan Award in 2009, provides state-of-the-art services for animal owners and referring practitioners. Although it is a big building, its form is cut into the landscape, the roof creating a new angled, grassed hillside and marrying the building into its parkland setting.

Internally, the building is simply organized both horizontally and vertically, with a clear division of public and private hospital space. The working hospital, held within the gabion wall, pinwheels around a central treatment hub, offering clear and unrestricted views towards the operational areas. Teaching and office spaces occupy the upper level, which has views over the estate and access on to the grass roof.

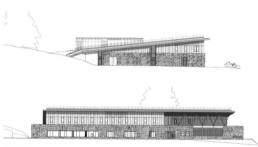

Sections

TRONGATE 103
TRONGATE, GLASGOW

ELDER & CANNON ARCHITECTS

CLIENT: GLASGOW CITY COUNCIL DEVELOPMENT AND REGENERATION SERVICES
STRUCTURAL ENGINEER: DEWAR ASSOCIATES
SERVICES ENGINEER: HENDERSON WARNOCK
CONTRACTOR: GRAHAM CONSTRUCTION
CONTRACT VALUE: £7,050,000
DATE OF COMPLETION: SEPTEMBER 2009
GROSS INTERNAL AREA: 7913 SQ. M
IMAGES: ELDER & CANNON ARCHITECTS (BOTTOM); GLASGOW CITY
      COUNCIL (TOP)

This was an extraordinarily complex conversion project, not just because of the multiple and opinionated end users, but also because it involved three listed buildings in varying states of disrepair. The clarity and quality of the public and studio spaces, and the use of natural lighting, are very impressive. This is a great asset for both the public and the artists who use the building.

Both the restoration work and the new interventions have been carried out with skill and rigour, and the distinction between the two is clearly made. The detailing throughout is excellent. The scheme will be an effective catalyst for Glasgow's planned Arts Quarter. This is true community architecture at its best.

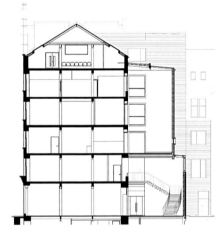

Section

DOWNE HOSPITAL
STRUELL WELLS ROAD, DOWNPATRICK

SCOTT WILSON

CLIENT: SOUTH EASTERN HEALTH AND SOCIAL CARE TRUST
STRUCTURAL ENGINEER: SCOTT WILSON
SERVICES ENGINEER: WHITE YOUNG GREEN
CONTRACTOR: MCLAUGHLIN & HARVEY
CONTRACT VALUE: £64,000,000
DATE OF COMPLETION: JUNE 2009
GROSS INTERNAL AREA: 22,222 SQ. M
IMAGES: RORY MOORE

The success of the new regional hospital is due to a clear-sighted client vision about making healthcare a welcoming experience, executed with straightforward, legible and uplifting architecture.

The new building departs from the original institutional form by breaking down the mass with an array of smaller wings springing from a central entrance. One benefit of disintegrating a large building into smaller architectural forms is the effect it has on the sense of well-being in the hospital's many rooms. All spaces are daylit and, where possible, they are naturally ventilated. This is not groundbreaking or heroic architecture, but it is a sophisticated response to a complex building type, which owes its success to a straightforward design that is welcoming and offers a sense of reassuring ease to its users.

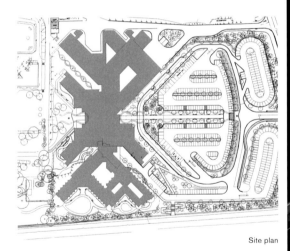

Site plan

KEVIN KAHAN SALON
HIGH STREET, BANGOR

TWENTY TWO OVER SEVEN

CLIENT: KEVIN KAHAN
STRUCTURAL ENGINEER: RPS BELFAST
SERVICES ENGINEER: WILLIAMS & SHAW
CONTRACTOR: MATHESON CONTRACTS
CONTRACT VALUE: £475,000
DATE OF COMPLETION: MAY 2008
GROSS INTERNAL AREA: 290 SQ. M
IMAGES: BIG GLASS EYE (LEFT); AIDAN MCGRATH (RIGHT)

This is an unexpected project for many reasons, partly because of the scale and depth of top-lit cavernous space quarried from the back yard behind a conventional terraced shopfront, but also because of the sheer success of such a huge salon in this location.

This is obviously a successful alliance between an entrepreneurial client and carefully crafted interior architecture. The sensitive control of natural and artificial light, a palette of very few materials, and an ensemble of well-proportioned and detailed moments, all make for a charming, pampering environment.

This space is intelligently engineered around the pragmatic workings of an efficient and award-winning hairdressing service, while also seeming intimately crafted around the bespoke requirements of its many repeat customers.

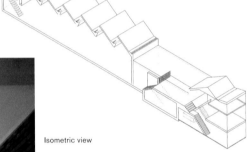

Isometric view

ST MALACHY'S CHURCH
ALFRED STREET, BELFAST

CONSARC CONSERVATION

CLIENT: FR ANTHONY CURRAN
STRUCTURAL ENGINEER: DORAN CONSULTING
SERVICES ENGINEER: WILLIAMS & SHAW
CONTRACTOR: O'NEILL & BRADY
CONTRACT VALUE: £3,000,000
DATE OF COMPLETION: APRIL 2009
GROSS INTERNAL AREA: 1272 SQ. M
IMAGES: CONSARC CONSERVATION

St Malachy's is a delightful early Victorian church characterized by its robust brick exterior with toy-Gothic turrets, and an elaborately plastered interior, which has been formed around a very unusual but intimate congregational organization on two levels.

The recent refurbishment has brought out the richness of the original painted colour scheme as well as restoring mosaics damaged by post-war alterations and brickwork that had suffered through years of weathering. A number of interventions, discreetly executed to meet such modern requirements as disabled access, improved heating and appropriate artificial lighting, do not detract from the original character, but rather add important comfort and amenity for the benefit of the congregation. They also draw attention to the beauty and humanity of the original building.

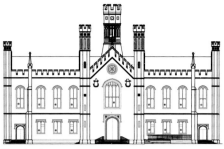

Front elevation

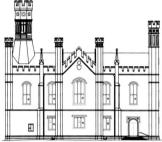

Side elevation

CITYSPACE
UNIVERSITY OF SUNDERLAND

FAULKNERBROWNS ARCHITECTS

CLIENT: UNIVERSITY OF SUNDERLAND
STRUCTURAL ENGINEER: BURO HAPPOLD
SERVICES ENGINEERS: ATKINS (PRE-NOVATION)/
    EMCOR GROUP; DTA CONSULTING ENGINEERS (POST-NOVATION)
CONTRACTOR: MORGAN ASHURST
CONTRACT VALUE: £12,000,000
DATE OF COMPLETION: SEPTEMBER 2009
GROSS INTERNAL AREA: 4034 SQ. M
IMAGES: MARTINE HAMILTON KNIGHT – ARCAID

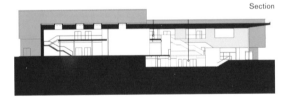

Section

This flagship university sports and leisure hub cleverly fuses
a complex architectural language on the main façade with an
understated robust treatment to the rest of the building. The main
effect is achieved by creating a massive, thick façade punctured
by seemingly random slots of green stained glass. This is a secular
cathedral to well-being, with facilities including gym and
performance spaces in addition to the main sports hall. This
impressive volume has no unnecessary details, but is well
considered: it is efficient and has character. A neat fold-away
seating system forms stadium seating for 450 people. The client is
convinced that the building sets a standard for Sunderland, both
architecturally and in terms of the inclusive programme.

COOPER'S STUDIOS
WESTGATE ROAD, NEWCASTLE UPON TYNE

RYDER ARCHITECTURE

CLIENT: THE HANRO GROUP
STRUCTURAL ENGINEER: EDWARD BIRD ASSOCIATES
SERVICES ENGINEER: SCREEN & FORSTER
CONTRACTOR: WHELAN
CONTRACT VALUE: £1,780,000
DATE OF COMPLETION: FEBRUARY 2009
GROSS INTERNAL AREA: 1,514 SQ. M
IMAGES: KRISTEN MCCLUSKIE

These Grade II-listed late-nineteenth-century livery stables have been stripped back to a shell, with new services woven around the ceiling, creating a layer of detail that is unashamedly basic.

However, the masterstroke of the project comes in the treatment of the façade, where four of the blank brick arches have been opened up and glazed. These triple-height frameless windows sit within Cor-ten steel reveals and create a clear juxtaposition with the renovated sash windows. In a move that is more reminiscent of the American architecture-trained artist Gordon Matta-Clark than English Heritage, the cross section of the building is revealed, and left, in the cut where the façade meets the floor slab. Meanwhile, the windows serve as a vitrine to a piece of architectural archaeology.

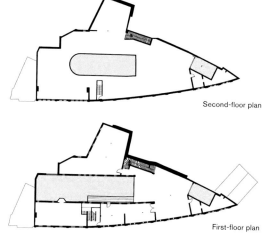

Second-floor plan

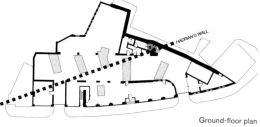

First-floor plan

Ground-floor plan

GREAT NORTH MUSEUM
BARRAS BRIDGE, NEWCASTLE UPON TYNE

FARRELLS; PURVES ASH

CLIENTS: NEWCASTLE UNIVERSITY WITH TYNE & WEAR ARCHIVES & MUSEUMS
STRUCTURAL ENGINEER: WSP
SERVICES ENGINEER: WHITE YOUNG GREEN
CONTRACTOR: KIER NORTH EAST
CONTRACT VALUE: £26,000,000
DATE OF COMPLETION: MAY 2009
GROSS INTERNAL AREA: 4500 SQ. M
IMAGES: ANDREW HASLAM

Restoration and a purpose-built wing have breathed new life into this unusual classical building. The architectural strategy was simple and clear: to pull out the detritus of a hundred years that had accumulated on walls, floors and ceiling, and to create new openings to allow uninterrupted circulation. Sensitive objects are housed in chemically controlled micro-environments, meaning that temperature fluctuations in the building are acceptable.

The new building was placed at the end of the enfilade and houses a tall gallery with flexible space, a second cafe, a library and administrative functions.

From the macro-scale of the building to the micro-scale of an exhibit, this museum provides an exciting thread of continuity that amazes and informs its public.

Elevation

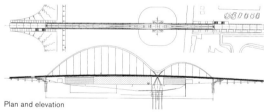

Plan and elevation

INFINITY BRIDGE
NORTHSHORE, STOCKTON-ON-TEES

SPENCE ASSOCIATES

CLIENT: STOCKTON-ON-TEES BOROUGH COUNCIL
STRUCTURAL ENGINEER: EXPEDITION ENGINEERING
CONTRACTOR: BALFOUR BEATTY CIVIL ENGINEERING
CONTRACT VALUE: £15,300,000
DATE OF COMPLETION: MAY 2008
IMAGE: MORLEY VON STERNBERG – ARCAID

This 180-metre-long bridge is extraordinarily slender, an almost one-dimensional arc, supported by a major and a minor bow. The cables are gathered beneath the concrete deck and post-tensioned by a pair of longitudinal cables. Ingeniously, these same cables also tie in the arches and prevent wobbling. It is more of an instrument than an inanimate object.

The project is the result of a collaboration between architect and engineer, and won an RIBA competition in 2003. The significance of the site is not to be overlooked: Margaret Thatcher was photographed here in 1987 'walking in the wilderness', a graphic demonstration of lost industry, community and place. The bridge, a beautifully constructed wiggle across the Tees, stands, therefore, as an inspiring beacon of hope.

NEWCASTLE CITY LIBRARY
NEW BRIDGE STREET WEST, NEWCASTLE UPON TYNE

RYDER ARCHITECTURE

CLIENT: NEWCASTLE CITY COUNCIL
STRUCTURAL ENGINEER: MOTT MACDONALD
SERVICES ENGINEER: SES
CONTRACTOR: TOLENT CONSTRUCTION
CONTRACT VALUE: £24,000,000
DATE OF COMPLETION: MARCH 2009
GROSS INTERNAL AREA: 8300 SQ. M
IMAGES: TIM CROCKER

The new city library replaces a well-loved but worn-out building designed by Basil Spence in the mid-1960s, and updates the whole concept of how a library can be a truly useful and inspiring community resource. An oblique view has the library peering out from the building line and making its presence felt well beyond its boundaries. The glass façade is decorated with a poetic motif generated from the collaboration between a local artist and local people.

A children's library area provides the right level of fun and learning for juniors and parents alike. There is a particularly special detail on the top floor: the rare books are housed in specially designed climate-conditioned cabinets in a slate box made of material salvaged from the old building.

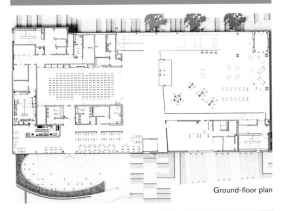
Ground-floor plan

CHIPS
LAMPWICK LANE, MANCHESTER

ALSOP ARCHITECTS

CLIENT: URBAN SPLASH
LANDSCAPE DESIGNER: GRANT ASSOCIATES
STRUCTURAL ENGINEER: MARTIN STOCKLEY ASSOCIATES
SERVICES ENGINEERS: QUARTZELEC; FULCRUM CONSULTING
CONTRACTOR: URBAN SPLASH BUILD
CONTRACT VALUE: £20,000,000
DATE OF COMPLETION: JUNE 2009
GROSS INTERNAL AREA: 16,200 SQ. M
IMAGES: CHRISTIAN RICHTERS – VIEW

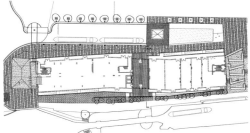

Elevation and ground-floor plan

Chips is a flagship for the New Islington area. The residential building's sculptural form and its strong graphic treatment create a striking architectural expression. This is what happens when such an architect as Will Alsop meets such a developer as Urban Splash: the structure is flamboyant, daring and also very big, more akin to one of the warehouses that hug the canals in these parts than some of the less successful attempts to house people in large numbers. It is the first part to be delivered of Alsop's own masterplan (a series of 'fingers' of accommodation and leisure alongside water); and perhaps also an Alsop finger to the housing establishment.

In Chips, clear decisions about the architectural issues at stake in the project have been made, and these decisions are pursued to an unusual conclusion.

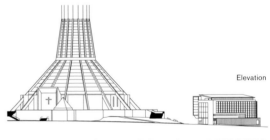

Elevation

LIVERPOOL JOHN MOORES UNIVERSITY ART AND DESIGN ACADEMY
DUCKINFIELD STREET, LIVERPOOL

RICK MATHER ARCHITECTS

CLIENT: LIVERPOOL JOHN MOORES UNIVERSITY
STRUCTURAL/SERVICES ENGINEER: RAMBOLL UK
CONTRACTOR: WATES CONSTRUCTION
CONTRACT VALUE: £24,000,000
DATE OF COMPLETION: DECEMBER 2008
GROSS INTERNAL AREA: 11,000 SQ. M
IMAGES: ANDY MATTHEWS – RICK MATHER ARCHITECTS (TOP); RICK MATHER
    ARCHITECTS (CENTRE; BOTTOM)
LONGLISTED FOR THE RIBA STIRLING PRIZE

Walking into the building, you get an immediate sense of activity: you look up, look down into the cafe, look either side, and you are instantly struck by an atmosphere of creativity.

The building's entrance and atrium are part of a sequence that forms a new public space and a link between the art school and Liverpool Metropolitan Cathedral. The building, set on a very tricky sloping site, balances a robust simplicity that suits the demands of environments for creative activity with moments of more complex spatial arrangements in public areas, such as the lobby, gallery space and lecture theatres. The architect has given the students an enviable new venue that is both practical and inspiring.

LIVERPOOL ONE, SITES 1 AND 7
LIVERPOOL

DIXON JONES; HAWORTH TOMPKINS

CLIENT: GROSVENOR
STRUCTURAL ENGINEER: WATERMAN GROUP
SERVICES ENGINEER: HOARE LEA
CONTRACTOR: BALFOUR BEATTY
CONTRACT VALUE: SITE 1 (DIXON JONES) £21,000,000;
    SITE 7 (HAWORTH TOMKINS) £15,200,000
DATE OF COMPLETION: OCTOBER 2008
GROSS INTERNAL AREA: 8255 SQ. M (SITE 1); 8867 SQ. M (SITE 7)
IMAGES: PAUL MCMULLIN (BOTTOM RIGHT); PAUL RAFTERY – VIEW (TOP);
    TIMOTHY SOAR (BOTTOM LEFT)

The project is an urban block with multiple authors, resulting in a building with rich architectural qualities. Part refurbishment, part social housing and part retail space, the block has a diversity of programmes and a range of architectural languages. The Dixon Jones arcade is a carefully considered experience, drawing on historical models that bring a grandeur and cultural texture to a contemporary retail offer. Haworth Tompkins uses a tough engineering brick for its tough housing. The unusual palette creates a variety of textures that respond to difference in contexts at particular moments.

Overall, the scheme suggests the possibility for a pluralistic architecture that can address social use while accommodating more luxurious sensations and experiences, both spatially and materially.

Elevation

NEW ROUNDHOUSE
ASHTON OLD ROAD, MANCHESTER

WALKER SIMPSON ARCHITECTS

CLIENTS: MANCHESTER SETTLEMENT; THE MANCHESTER COLLEGE;
    MOSSCARE HOUSING
STRUCTURAL ENGINEER: SHEPHERD GILMOUR
SERVICES ENGINEER: ENVIRONMENTAL SERVICES DESIGN (FORMERLY
    OPERON)
CONTRACTOR: J. GREENWOOD BUILDERS
CONTRACT VALUE: £1,690,000
DATE OF COMPLETION: JUNE 2009
GROSS INTERNAL AREA: 1000 SQ. M
IMAGES: DANIEL HOPKINSON – ARCAID

Externally, the building creates a strong civic presence, an important quality in an area that is going through large-scale regeneration. Its simplicity of form and material lends a positive appearance.

The elevation had to negotiate the wish of the client (an education, housing and legal-advice charity) for both visible presence in the community and privacy for the building's users. The exterior balances these needs by creating larger openings at a higher level.

The building is organized around an atrium that is derived from the desire to create a naturally ventilated building. The atrium is positioned off-centre in plan and gives the building an interesting interior spatial quality, linking the project's different activities as well as offering glimpses through and beyond the scheme.

Section

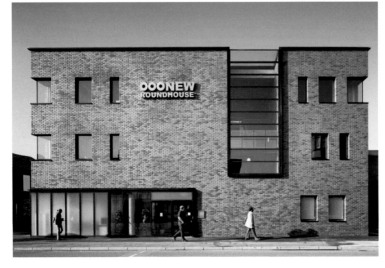

BROADCASTING PLACE
WOODHOUSE LANE, LEEDS

FEILDEN CLEGG BRADLEY STUDIOS

CLIENT: DOWNING
STRUCTURAL ENGINEER: HALCROW YOLLES
SERVICES ENGINEER: KGA PARTNERSHIP
CONTRACTOR: GEORGE DOWNING CONSTRUCTION
CONTRACT VALUE: £50,000,000
DATE OF COMPLETION: OCTOBER 2009
GROSS INTERNAL AREA: 21,600 SQ. M
IMAGES: WILL PRYCE

This complex of buildings for Leeds Metropolitan University works cleverly at many levels. It stands on the ridge above central Leeds in the university quarter, which already has a number of well-known towers. The scale varies from the two storeys of the retained building to the twenty-three-storey student residential tower, which is a truly iconic addition to the cityscape and presents its sculpted narrow edge to the city centre; its shape and the Cor-ten steel cladding make reference to Yorkshire's rugged landscape.

The many constraints and uses have been skilfully handled. The uses include teaching spaces, arts studio spaces, offices, a Baptist church and accommodation for 240 students. These are all well-planned, legible functions. A BREEAM 'Very Good' rating has been achieved.

Elevation

HULL TRUCK THEATRE
FERENSWAY, HULL

WRIGHT & WRIGHT ARCHITECTS

CLIENT: HULL TRUCK ENTERPRISES
STRUCTURAL ENGINEER: ALAN BAXTER & ASSOCIATES
SERVICES ENGINEER: MAX FORDHAM
CONTRACTOR: QUARMBY CONSTRUCTION
CONTRACT VALUE: £10,500,000
DATE OF COMPLETION: MARCH 2009
GROSS INTERNAL AREA: 4050 SQ. M
IMAGES: PETER COOK – VIEW

The opportunity to construct a purpose-built theatre that could take on board the inclusive culture of this unique company, which had been shaped in part by its inadequate premises, was a challenge that both the architect and the client have clearly relished.

The theatre foyer opens straight on to the street and invites in the public, whether theatregoers or not. The building includes educational facilities as well as a main auditorium seating 440 and a studio space for 134. The theatre has a rugged, gritty seaport heritage, and the architect has reflected that in the robust forms and detailing, delivering a sculpted, dark-brick box with shipbuilding-quality steel detailing. In contrast, the auditorium seats are luxuriously comfortable.

This is a great architectural response to a complex physical brief and an even more challenging programme.

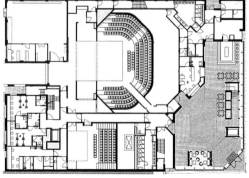

Ground-floor plan

JUNCTION
PARADISE PLACE, GOOLE

BUSCHOW HENLEY

CLIENT: GOOLE TOWN COUNCIL
STRUCTURAL ENGINEER: TECHNIKER
SERVICES ENGINEER: RYB KONSULT GROUP
THEATRE CONSULTANTS: THEATREPLAN
CONTRACTOR: GEO. HOULTON & SONS
CONTRACT VALUE: £2,450,000
DATE OF COMPLETION: 2009
GROSS INTERNAL AREA: 1300 SQ. M
IMAGES: ANDREW HASLAM

Junction is in a complex urban situation. It is an edge building on the side of a relatively new space called Wesley Square, but it also links back to the earlier shopping areas of Goole. Its programme is a wonderful mixture of community uses: an arts centre containing a 170-seat auditorium that can also be used as a cinema and performance workshop, a community centre and cafe, a covered market area and the town council offices – all remarkably contained within a gross area of 1300 square metres.

The really clever thing about the complex is that it is constructed around a retained steel frame and ground slab left over from a 1980s extension to the Victorian market next door.

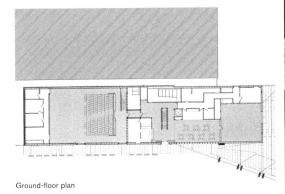

Ground-floor plan

NAVIGATION WAREHOUSE
WAKEFIELD WATERFRONT

BDP

CLIENT: CTP ST JAMES
STRUCTURAL ENGINEER: SEJC CONSULTING ENGINEERS
SERVICES ENGINEER: ERNEST GRIFFITHS & SONS
CONTRACTOR: WILLIAM ANELAY
CONTRACT VALUE: £24,000,000
DATE OF COMPLETION: 2009
GROSS INTERNAL AREA: 2400 SQ. M
IMAGES: MARTINE HAMILTON KNIGHT – ARCAID

The Grade II*-listed Navigation Warehouse, dating from 1792, had been derelict for more than twenty-five years. It comprises two main ranges perpendicular to the river, with a smaller one in between. This element had virtually collapsed.

The external walls of the interface building have been faithfully reconstructed, but the inside is an elegant contemporary intervention that provides the elements needed by office occupation: an accommodation staircase, a fire escape, toilets and a lift. The contemporary design is made up of steel, oak and glass, and the whole central area is top-lit by a new glazed rooflight. This space provides natural stack-effect ventilation to the adjacent office spaces, which have opening windows, while a new highly thermally efficient roof has been installed.

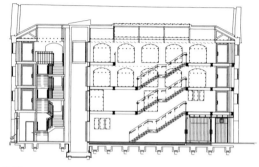

Section

THE WORKSHOP STUDIO
NETHER EDGE, SHEFFIELD

DRDH ARCHITECTS

CLIENT: THE WORKSHOP
STRUCTURAL ENGINEER: ROLTON GROUP
SERVICES ENGINEER: JSH CONSULTING
CONTRACTOR: GRAHAM STUART CONSTRUCTION
CONTRACT VALUE: £599,000
DATE OF COMPLETION: JANUARY 2008
GROSS INTERNAL AREA: 958 SQ. M
IMAGES: DAVID GRANDORGE

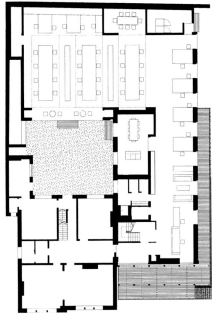

This well-proportioned suburban house had received an incongruous two-storey extension in the 1960s and has been used for business purposes ever since. The architect's task was to transform and extend the building to house The Workshop, a design and communications consultancy employing fifty staff.

The extension was refaced with red sandstone and remodelled with a classically elegant portico made of bronze anodized aluminium box-sections. As a direct result of the quality of the planning and the execution of the project, there is a sense of calm about the place despite fairly high occupancy. The existing and new buildings define a beautiful internal courtyard, which is used as the setting for lunches and barbecues. This is a sublimely crafted piece of work.

Ground-floor plan

CARDIFF CENTRAL LIBRARY
THE HAYES, CARDIFF

BDP

CLIENTS: CARDIFF COUNTY COUNCIL; ST DAVID'S PARTNERSHIP
STRUCTURAL ENGINEER: ARUP
SERVICES ENGINEER: FOREMAN ROBERTS
CONTRACTOR: LAING O'ROURKE
CONTRACT VALUE: £18,000,000
DATE OF COMPLETION: APRIL 2009
GROSS INTERNAL AREA: 5167 SQ. M
IMAGES: DAVID BARBOUR – BDP

The bold and colourful Cardiff Central Library sits at the convergence of two pedestrianized streets. The ground-floor foyer is modest, so as to encourage the use of the escalators that rise through a lofty linear atrium – a theatrical arrival sequence that allows the visitor time to take in their surroundings and orientate themselves. At the very top, the library is crowned with a warm timber ceiling, laid out on a grid that cuts across the atrium and reinforces the building plan, which is dynamic and sophisticated.

The library was opened by the Welsh rock band the Manic Street Preachers, whose lyric 'Libraries gave us power' is quoted on the commemorative plaque. It is an appropriate sentiment for a striking and accessible new public library.

Sections

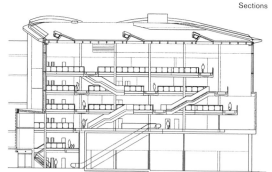

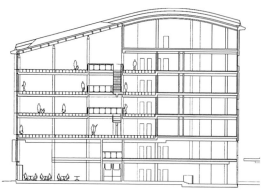

CHAPTER
MARKET ROAD, CANTON, CARDIFF

ASH SAKULA ARCHITECTS

CLIENT: CHAPTER
STRUCTURAL ENGINEER: ADAMS KARA TAYLOR
SERVICES ENGINEER: MICHAEL POPPER ASSOCIATES
CONTRACTOR: WRW GROUP
CONTRACT VALUE: £2,240,000
DATE OF COMPLETION: NOVEMBER 2009
GROSS INTERNAL AREA: 3991 SQ. M
IMAGES: JON POUNTNEY (LEFT); ASH SAKULA (RIGHT)

The brief required the rationalization of Chapter's existing buildings without the loss of the sometimes eccentric qualities that have made it a highly successful centre for the visual and performing arts and a Cardiff institution since its inception in the early 1970s.

In an inspired reversal, a previously open courtyard has been covered to create a cafe/bar that is bright, airy and constantly animated by visitors. Despite a low budget, spaces are of uniformly high quality. New finishes are full of character, and the building reveals many delightful details – such as putty-green panelling and chocolate-coloured ceramic dado tiles – uncovered from behind layers of paint and plasterboard. There is even a low-budget homage to Gunnar Asplund's seminal 1920s Skandia Cinema in Stockholm, with red velvet seats and a fibre-optic night-sky ceiling.

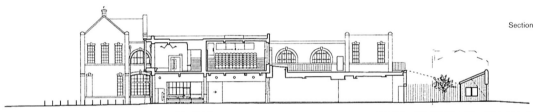

Section

CREATIVE BUSINESS UNITS
ABERYSTWYTH ARTS CENTRE, ABERYSTWYTH UNIVERSITY

HEATHERWICK STUDIO

CLIENT: ABERYSTWYTH ARTS CENTRE
STRUCTURAL ENGINEER: PACKMAN LUCAS
SERVICES ENGINEER: ADRIAN TESTER
CONTRACTOR: HEATHERWICK STUDIO
CONTRACT VALUE: £1,150,000
DATE OF COMPLETION: JANUARY 2009
GROSS INTERNAL AREA: 624 SQ. M
IMAGES: EDMUND SUMNER – VIEW

This RIBA competition-winning project for Aberystwyth Arts Centre provides sixteen small creative business starter units set along a gently meandering path on a wooded hillside overlooking the sea.

The interiors of the 39-square-metre units are modest, in stunning contrast to their exteriors, which appear to be clad in shiny inflated 'pillows' that reflect the colours of the surrounding trees and sky. These plump, creased forms are in fact hard and durable, and formed of wafer-thin sheets of stainless steel – pre-creased by a bespoke hand-operated 'mangle' invented by the architect – coated on the reverse with two types of CFC-free insulation foam, which brings thermal performance and rigidity. The effect is extraordinary, and simultaneously intriguing and charming.

Section, elevation and plan

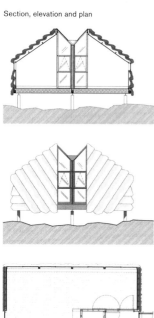

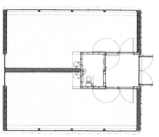

HAFOD ERYRI
(SNOWDON SUMMIT BUILDING)
YR WYDDFA (SNOWDON)

RAY HOLE ARCHITECTS

CLIENT: SNOWDONIA NATIONAL PARK AUTHORITY
STRUCTURAL/SERVICES ENGINEER: ARUP
CONTRACTOR: CARILLION
CONTRACT VALUE: £7,300,000
DATE OF COMPLETION: OCTOBER 2008
GROSS INTERNAL AREA: 700 SQ. M
IMAGES: RAY WOOD

It is rare in the modern era to describe a building as heroic, yet the visitor centre at the summit of Snowdon truly deserves that accolade. No other building in the United Kingdom has been built at such high altitude, and it was designed to withstand an extreme climate and high visitor numbers.

Before being taken to the site, the galvanized-steel-framed building was completely pre-assembled to resolve any problems of fit and tolerance. It was then clad in an aluminium standing-seam enclosure and enveloped in roughly hewn granite blocks. This is an extraordinary contextual building that is completely at one with its uniquely sensitive setting, and which – because it forms the summer terminus for the Snowdon Mountain Railway – brings Wales's most symbolic mountain within reach for everyone without compromising the mountain or the enjoyment of it.

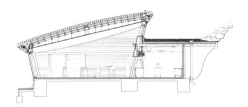

Section

MARGAM DISCOVERY CENTRE
MARGAM COUNTRY PARK, PORT TALBOT

LOYN & CO. ARCHITECTS;
DESIGN RESEARCH UNIT WALES

CLIENT: NEATH PORT TALBOT COUNTY BOROUGH COUNCIL
STRUCTURAL/SERVICES ENGINEER: AECOM
CONTRACTOR: WRW GROUP
CONTRACT VALUE: £4,900,000
DATE OF COMPLETION: MARCH 2009
GROSS INTERNAL AREA: 3138 SQ. M
IMAGES: DESIGN RESEARCH UNIT WALES (BOTTOM); KIRAN RIDLEY (TOP)

Some 80 per cent of this experimental building was prefabricated as modular units and craned into position, although the building module is visible only in vertical joints in the timber cladding. The research into this sustainable educational, cultural and leisure facility was undertaken by the Welsh School of Architecture's Design Research Unit, in collaboration with local architecture firm Loyn & Co.

The building plays a didactic role in demonstrating sustainable design to users, incorporating passive design strategies, biomass plant and water recycling. It also provides a base from which to explore the history, culture and ecology of the surrounding landscape.

The architectural form reinforces these aims, with the building set on 'piloti' (in fact, drilling tubes recycled from the oil industry) so that it literally treads lightly on the earth.

Elevation

SKYPAD: TEENAGE CANCER TRUST UNIT CARDIFF
UNIVERSITY HOSPITAL OF WALES, HEATH PARK, CARDIFF

ORMS ARCHITECTURE DESIGN

CLIENTS: TEENAGE CANCER TRUST; CARDIFF & VALE UNIVERSITY HEALTH
    BOARD
STRUCTURAL ENGINEER: PRICE & MYERS
SERVICES ENGINEER: AECOM
CONTRACTOR: COWLIN CONSTRUCTION
CONTRACT VALUE: £2,400,000
DATE OF COMPLETION: MAY 2009
GROSS INTERNAL AREA: 585 SQ. M
IMAGES: JAMES BRITTAIN – VIEW

This extraordinary project can take its rightful place among a series of landmark healthcare buildings, including Alvar Aalto's Paimio Sanatorium (an explicit point of reference for the architect), that use sensitive, humane design to improve the physical and emotional environment for patient care.

The architect has drawn on previous experience in hotel design to provide attractive and customizable interiors for the treatment of young people with cancer. The two-storey building is on a well-placed but highly constrained, landlocked site. The distinctive blue metal-clad form is supported on inclined tubular legs, a familiar architectural device that here is driven by necessity, to step nimbly over myriad existing services, ventilation outlets and fire-escape routes and to connect directly to existing adult and paediatric oncology services.

Isometric sketch

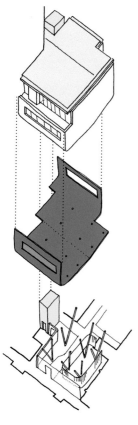

SLEEPERZ HOTEL
STATION APPROACH, SAUNDERS ROAD, CARDIFF

CLASH ARCHITECTS; HOLDER MATHIAS ARCHITECTS

CLIENT: SLEEPERZ HOTELS
STRUCTURAL ENGINEERS: TECHNIKER; RVW CONSULTING
SERVICES ENGINEERS: HULLEY & KIRKWOOD; NEPTUNE BUILDING SERVICES
CONTRACTOR: COWLIN CONSTRUCTION
CONTRACT VALUE: £4,622,010
DATE OF COMPLETION: NOVEMBER 2008
GROSS INTERNAL AREA: 1632 SQ. M
IMAGES: DANIEL CLEMENTS – VIEW

The 350-square-metre triangular site near Cardiff Central Station
lay empty for fifteen years and contributed to an air of neglect.
The enterprising development of a bold new seventy-four-bed hotel
acts as a high-quality catalyst for the regeneration of the wider area.

The planners insisted on the use of real stone, and this shifted
the project from a budget hotel towards a boutique destination.
Even so, the construction cost per room is lower than even for
budget providers, suggesting that many more locations could be
made to work with this sort of thinking and with clever design
tailored to small sites. This is not back-to-basics architecture,
but possibly a reinvention of the city-centre hotel model for a
money-conscious world.

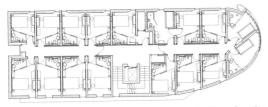

Typical upper-floor plan

ZERO-CARBON HOUSE
TINDAL STREET, BIRMINGHAM

JOHN CHRISTOPHERS

CLIENTS: JO HINDLEY AND JOHN CHRISTOPHERS
STRUCTURAL ENGINEER: SHIRE CONSULTING
ENVIRONMENTAL DESIGN CONSULTANT: LEDA
CONTRACTOR: SPELLER METCALFE
CONTRACT VALUE: £350,000
DATE OF COMPLETION: NOVEMBER 2009
GROSS INTERNAL AREA: 204 SQ. M
IMAGES: MARTINE HAMILTON KNIGHT – ARCAID
SHORTLISTED FOR THE RIBA MANSER MEDAL

John Christophers, past winner of the RIBA Sustainability Award
and associate of Associated Architects, has transformed an existing
end-of-terrace house into a family home of rare quality using low-
energy materials and environmental systems. It is the United
Kingdom's first retrofit house to achieve zero carbon standards as
defined in the Code for Sustainable Homes Level 6; in fact, thanks
to solar thermal and PV panels and a heat-recovery system, the
family hardly needed to light the wood-burning stove throughout an
extremely cold winter.

Externally, the house has a completely different character from
the rest of the area, but really adds to the urban streetscape. It is
full of quirky, delightful and well-considered details, and is a robust
and thoughtful design of exceptional quality.

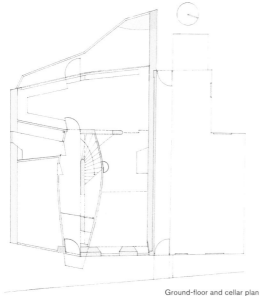

Ground-floor and cellar plan

MUSEUM COURT
GRANTHAM STREET, LINCOLN

JONATHAN HENDRY ARCHITECTS

CLIENT: STRAIT DEVELOPMENT
STRUCTURAL/SERVICES ENGINEER: BWB CONSULTING
ARCHAEOLOGICAL SERVICES: ARCHAEOLOGICAL PROJECT SERVICES
CONTRACTOR: ROBERT WOODHEAD
CONTRACT VALUE: £2,400,000
DATE OF COMPLETION: JANUARY 2009
GROSS INTERNAL AREA: 1677 SQ. M
IMAGES: DAVID GRANDORGE

The brief was both simple and challenging: build as many flats
as feasible on a difficult city-centre site. Add a tight budget, some
listed buildings, a steep incline and a housing market in decline,
and you could have a problem rather than the quietly impressive
scheme that Jonathan Hendry has designed for his developer client.
Through a deft handling of scale and proportion, the result
suggests a medieval street pattern. It is redolent of the forms and
textures of historic buildings, without any of the usual quotations or
period details. These simple, restrained buildings lend the scheme
a timeless air, with a few details that add an edge and give a
presence to the city beyond.

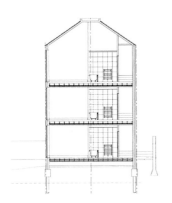

Sections

NOTTINGHAM CONTEMPORARY
WEEKDAY CROSS, NOTTINGHAM

CARUSO ST JOHN ARCHITECTS

CLIENT: NOTTINGHAM CITY COUNCIL
STRUCTURAL ENGINEERS: ARUP; ELLIOTT WOOD PARTNERSHIP
SERVICES ENGINEER: ARUP
CONTRACTOR: SOL CONSTRUCTION
CONTRACT VALUE: £12,300,000
DATE OF COMPLETION: NOVEMBER 2009
GROSS INTERNAL AREA: 3400 SQ. M
IMAGES: HÉLÈNE BINET
LONGLISTED FOR THE RIBA STIRLING PRIZE

Nottingham's new gallery, occupying a difficult, steeply sloping site, demands to be noticed. It signals itself with gold-plated towers that sit among the church spires and tall warehouses of the city's old Lace Market. Closer up, we see the wrap of scalloped green-grey concrete cladding with its delicate imprints. This building is special – it's different.

Nottingham Contemporary is thought-provoking, sensuous, clever and well suited to the purpose: to bring contemporary art to a wider audience. But one also feels the weight of this building: the concrete internal spaces feel hewn out of this place. This is a gallery with a presence that allows it to compete on an international scale; it has put Nottingham on the map.

Elevation

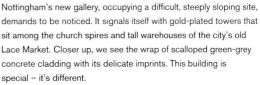

THINK TANK
RUSTON WAY, LINCOLN

MARKS BARFIELD ARCHITECTS

CLIENT: CITY OF LINCOLN COUNCIL
STRUCTURAL ENGINEER: JACOBS UK
SERVICES ENGINEER: XC02
CONTRACTOR: MARRIOTT CONSTRUCTION
CONTRACT VALUE: £7,100,000
DATE OF COMPLETION: JUNE 2009
GROSS INTERNAL AREA: 3525 SQ. M
IMAGES: IAN LAMBOT (BOTTOM LEFT AND RIGHT); PAUL RIDDLE – VIEW (TOP)

The brief was to provide a mixture of office and workshop spaces for small enterprises for short-term rent by the city council, in order to encourage start-up 'innovative' businesses. Think Tank offers this provision, but also gives a 'front' for new businesses that conveys professionalism, solidity and a dash of verve.

It is a building that encloses space, but is also open to the outside. There is a feeling that participation from the city outside is encouraged, while a sense of belonging is fostered within.

The finishes are surprising, jumping from concrete to timber to the chameleon skin, anchored by an organization and a relationship to the site that are simple and bold. There is a drama to each elevation that is expressive and arresting.

Ground-floor plan

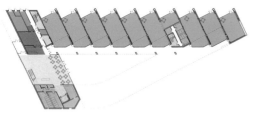

ALDEBURGH MUSIC CREATIVE CAMPUS
SNAPE MALTINGS, SUFFOLK

HAWORTH TOMPKINS

CLIENT: ALDEBURGH MUSIC
STRUCTURAL ENGINEER: PRICE & MYERS
SERVICES ENGINEER: E3 CONSULTING ENGINEERS
THEATRE CONSULTANT: CHARCOALBLUE
CONTRACTOR: HAYMILLS
CONTRACT VALUE: £5,500,000
DATE OF COMPLETION: MAY 2009
GROSS INTERNAL AREA: 2130 SQ. M
IMAGES: PHILIP VILE
LONGLISTED FOR THE RIBA STIRLING PRIZE AND SHORTLISTED FOR THE
     CROWN ESTATE CONSERVATION AWARD
ALDEBURGH MUSIC WAS SHORTLISTED FOR THE RIBA CLIENT OF THE YEAR

The main space in the new development at Snape Maltings, the Britten Studio, is breathtaking in its simplicity, invention and artistic concern with materiality. It takes the relatively sombre and simple architecture of the original Maltings by Arup and develops a more sophisticated level of detail. Throughout the complex series of technical-support and rehearsal spaces in the 'Creative Campus', each building element has been considered and either retained, altered, framed or reframed to maintain a dialogue between the industrial past and a sophisticated, cultured present.

The new clarity and intellectual edge of the Creative Campus are a masterclass in the innovative act of refurbishment, where the architect is very consciously selecting and evaluating, almost 'curating', the remaining fabric of a historic building.

Section

CREATIVE EXCHANGE
LONGSANDS CAMPUS, ST NEOTS

5TH STUDIO

CLIENT: HUNTINGDONSHIRE DISTRICT COUNCIL
STRUCTURAL ENGINEER: SCOTT WILSON
SERVICES ENGINEER: ZEF
CONTRACTOR: SDC SPECIAL PROJECTS
CONTRACT VALUE: £1,530,000
DATE OF COMPLETION: JANUARY 2009
GROSS INTERNAL AREA: 705 SQ. M
IMAGES: TIMOTHY SOAR

This extraordinary and intriguing building is an entirely appropriate response to the issues of business development in the rural context of Cambridgeshire.

The building form is complex. Each floorplate and each elevation creates a distinct 'place' for a small business. The experience is of an exhilarating tree house from which the occupants look down on the children rushing to and from Longsands College.

The choice of materials and fixings is strongly influenced by the budget, but also displays a touch of 'Hoxton chic', with such experimental materials as structural glass, second-hand plywood linings and face-fixed services. The energy strategy has surprising innovations, such as a buried earth pipe that provides cooled or warmed air, thus reducing energy costs.

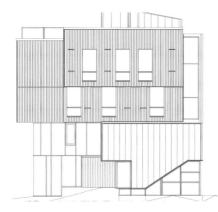

Elevation

DOWNING COLLEGE
REGENT STREET, CAMBRIDGE

CARUSO ST JOHN ARCHITECTS

CLIENT: DOWNING COLLEGE
STRUCTURAL ENGINEER: ALAN BAXTER & ASSOCIATES
SERVICES ENGINEERS: WSP INTEGRATED BUILDING SERVICES; MAX FORDHAM
CONSERVATION CONSULTANT: ALAN BAXTER & ASSOCIATES
CONTRACTOR: YORK CONSTRUCTION
CONTRACT VALUE: £4,680,000
DATE OF COMPLETION: JANUARY 2009
GROSS INTERNAL AREA: 1890 SQ. M
IMAGES: IOANA MARINESCU

Caruso St John has been working on Downing College's dining hall by William Wilkins and the adjacent buildings by Howell, Killick, Partridge and Amis since 2001.

The architect's response to the repair and extension of the 1960s building has involved the same care in matching materials and forms as has been applied to the considerations and evolution of the dining hall.

The college is delighted with the architect's intellectual engagement and the use of a language of materials, rhythms and scale to separate and link the 1960s buildings, the new spaces and the dining hall. It is surprising just how much of the convincingly 'historic' interior design by Caruso St John is in fact new structure.

Section

MARTELLO TOWER Y
BAWDSEY, SUFFOLK

**PIERCY CONNER ARCHITECTS
WITH BILLINGS JACKSON DESIGN**

CLIENTS: DUNCAN AND KRISTIN JACKSON
STRUCTURAL ENGINEERS: PRICE & MYERS; J.P. CHICK & PARTNERS
SERVICES ENGINEER: NORMAN DISNEY & YOUNG
CONTRACTORS: ROSEWOODS; SIMON GASKIN
CONTRACT VALUE: £400,000
DATE OF COMPLETION: JANUARY 2010
GROSS INTERNAL AREA: 120 SQ. M
IMAGES: EDMUND SUMNER – VIEW
SHORTLISTED FOR THE RIBA MANSER MEDAL AND
    THE STEPHEN LAWRENCE PRIZE

The Martello tower presents perhaps the ultimate challenge to the housing architect. The problems are manifold. From the bureaucratic point of view, one has to consider how to deal with a scheduled ancient monument (in this instance, one also on the at-risk register and in a designated Area of Outstanding Natural Beauty), and how to capture the magnificent views from the rooftop platform when heritage advisers deny enclosure. Then there is the question of how to introduce services into a structure that has 4-metre-thick walls, in a way that is both elegant and unobtrusive. And finally, the architect has to design in a way that sees the shape as an advantage, not a hindrance, to creativity. Here, the architects' sensitive response is typified by the beauty of the exposed domed brickwork and the indoor–outdoor roof terrace, which is oversailed but not enclosed.

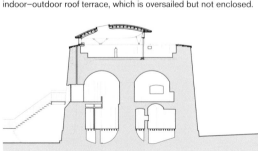

Section

NORWICH CATHEDRAL HOSTRY
THE CLOSE, NORWICH

HOPKINS ARCHITECTS WITH HENRY FREELAND, ARCHITECT TO NORWICH CATHEDRAL

CLIENT: NORWICH CATHEDRAL
STRUCTURAL ENGINEERS: BURO HAPPOLD; PHILIP COOPER
SERVICES ENGINEER: AECOM (FORMERLY FABER MAUNSELL)
CONTRACTOR: MORGAN ASHURST
CONTRACT VALUE: £12,500,000 (PHASES 1 AND 2)
DATE OF COMPLETION: NOVEMBER 2009
GROSS INTERNAL AREA: 1078 SQ. M
IMAGES: JAMES O'DAVIES (BOTTOM RIGHT); PAUL TYAGI (TOP; BOTTOM LEFT)
SHORTLISTED FOR THE CROWN ESTATE CONSERVATION AWARD

Hopkins won this job in a competition in the late 1990s. Uniquely, the proposal for the Refectory (completed in 2004) and the Hostry built new walls off the outline of existing walls and reused the existing spaces on the upper level of the existing cloister. This enables the scheme to match the massing and roof forms of the original cloister and to reinstate its relationship to the cathedral.

The project has an economy of means and a modesty in profile, balanced by an exuberance in the detailing. The architect has brought forward the materiality and the detailing of junctions from the Refectory while creating new spaces and responding to different needs, producing a satisfying and convincing scheme to bring the cathedral back to life.

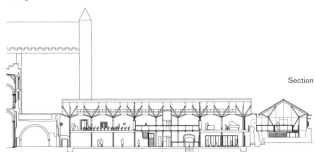

Section

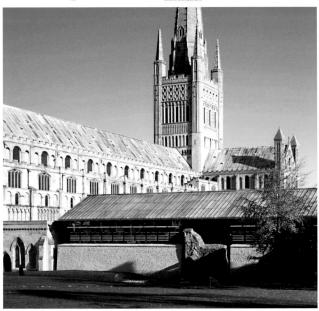

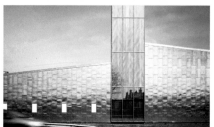

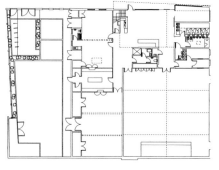

THE SALVATION ARMY CHELMSFORD
BADDOW ROAD, CHELMSFORD

HUDSON ARCHITECTS

CLIENT: THE SALVATION ARMY CHELMSFORD
STRUCTURAL ENGINEER: CURTINS CONSULTING
SERVICES ENGINEER: EP CONSULTING
CONTRACTOR: APOLLO GROUP
CONTRACT VALUE: £2,000,000
DATE OF COMPLETION: FEBRUARY 2009
GROSS INTERNAL AREA: 900 SQ. M
IMAGES: KEITH COLLIE
LONGLISTED FOR THE RIBA STIRLING PRIZE

With a limited budget and straightforward materials, the architect has made every space inside and outside the building say something. The interiors are well fitted to the busy, changing programme of the building's daily activities. The careful use of heat and light supports the modest, human uses in a way that demonstrates convincing and low-key sustainability.

Outside, the building makes great efforts to transform this run-down area of Chelmsford. The courtyard next to it could have been left open – forever a gap in the urban fabric – but instead a walled garden has been created to repair the building line. One magical element is the use of sunlight to project the image of the tower's cross on to the busy road.

Ground-floor plan

LEWIS HOUSE
WONFORD ROAD, EXETER

DAVID SHEPPARD ARCHITECTS

CLIENTS: MR AND MRS LEWIS
STRUCTURAL ENGINEER: STRUCTURAL SOLUTIONS
CONTRACTOR: IMPERIAL CONSTRUCTION
CONTRACT VALUE: £282,000
DATE OF COMPLETION: JULY 2009
GROSS INTERNAL AREA: 185 SQ. M
IMAGES: RD54

In this house in a Georgian suburb of Exeter, a lightweight wooden box floats above a necklace of clear and opaque glass, which separates the upper floor from the heavy rendered base of the lower storey. This light and airy ground floor has fully glazed retractable screens leading from open-plan sitting, dining and kitchen areas into a beautiful mature walled garden.

Voids cut into the floor and a mirror by the stairs create intricate and unexpected views that connect ground-and first-floor living areas. The quite intricate but relaxed interrelation of spaces seems to work really well for the family who live there. This unashamedly contemporary house within a conservation area gets good marks for its planners, its clients and its architect.

Section

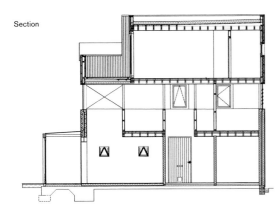

MILLS BAKERY
ROYAL WILLIAM YARD, PLYMOUTH

GILLESPIE YUNNIE ARCHITECTS

CLIENT: URBAN SPLASH
STRUCTURAL ENGINEER: HYDROCK STRUCTURES 1
SERVICES ENGINEER: HOARE LEA
CONTRACTOR: URBAN SPLASH BUILD
CONTRACT VALUE: £15,500,000
DATE OF COMPLETION: DECEMBER 2009
GROSS INTERNAL AREA: 11,000 SQ. M
IMAGES: PAUL GROOM (BOTTOM); JOHNATHAN MOORE (TOP LEFT AND RIGHT)

Mills Bakery forms part of the extraordinary South West Regional Development Agency/Urban Splash initiative to bring back into use Sir John Rennie's magnificent Grade I-listed Royal William Yard in Plymouth. The complex now provides 4000 square metres of commercial space and eighty-three flats.

Dramatic top-lit atria bring light and ventilation into the heart of the building and create delightful shared social spaces for the people who live and work there.

Conventional apartment layouts have been ditched in favour of quirky and bespoke designs that work with the constraints and opportunities presented by the former bakery's massive timber and cast-iron structure, which is exposed wherever possible. Beautifully detailed contemporary interventions in glass, steel and timber are juxtaposed with the historic building.

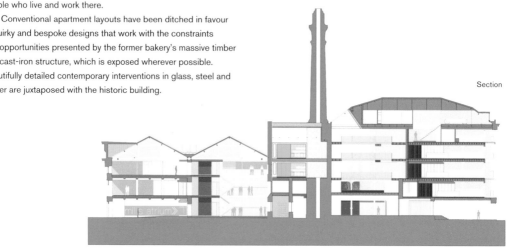

Section

AARDMAN ANIMATIONS HEADQUARTERS
GAS FERRY ROAD, BRISTOL

ALEC FRENCH ARCHITECTS

CLIENT: AARDMAN ANIMATIONS
STRUCTURAL/SERVICES ENGINEER: ARUP
CONTRACTOR: LEADBITTER CONSTRUCTION
CONTRACT VALUE: £7,700,000
DATE OF COMPLETION: FEBRUARY 2009
GROSS INTERNAL AREA: 3321 SQ. M
IMAGES: SIMON DOLING

Aardman's new headquarters consists of over 3000 square metres of light and airy workspace and a little cinema and cafe. Everything is arranged around a tapering three-storey atrium that houses a reception, semi-open meeting areas, wide bridges and landings/walkways that flow into work areas on either side. These are neither quite open nor quite cellular; walls are two-thirds height – high enough to make you feel enclosed when you're sitting down and low enough to enable a conversation with your neighbour if you're standing. The novel idea typifies the Aardman culture, just as the building as a whole demonstrates a spatiality that exerts a subtle, benign influence on its occupants.

The building's generosity extends outside, with display-cabinet windows signalling Aardman's presence to the street.

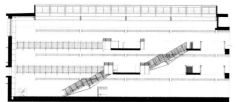

Section

FURZEY HALL FARM
GLOUCESTERSHIRE

WAUGH THISTLETON ARCHITECTS

CLIENT: PRIVATE
STRUCTURAL ENGINEER: ELLIOTT WOOD PARTNERSHIP
SERVICES ENGINEER: MICHAEL POPPER ASSOCIATES
CONTRACTOR: MS BUILDING & RENOVATION
CONTRACT VALUE: CONFIDENTIAL
DATE OF COMPLETION: JUNE 2009
GROSS INTERNAL AREA: 442 SQ. M
IMAGES: WILL PRYCE
SHORTLISTED FOR THE RIBA MANSER MEDAL

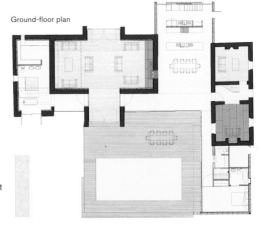

Ground-floor plan

The project involved the restoration of a Victorian Cotswold-stone farmhouse and an adjacent barn. These are now linked by an elegant L-shaped single-storey timber-and-glass building that frames two sides of the garden; inside is a generous open-plan kitchen/dining area, which opens on to a decked terrace and a swimming pool that is filtered by a reed bed. The barn houses spectacular double-height living spaces, a quirky open-plan bathroom and metal stairs leading to a mezzanine bedroom.

The thick rubblework exterior walls of the existing farmhouse, now absorbed into the interior of the house, are a delightful contrast to the smooth, minimal finishes of the new building. Ground-source heat pumps provide heating and hot water.

THE HYDE
DILLINGTON, SOMERSET

PURCELL MILLER TRITTON

CLIENT: WAYNE BENNETT, DILLINGTON HOUSE, SOMERSET
STRUCTURAL ENGINEER: HYDER CONSULTING
SERVICES ENGINEER: AECOM
CONTRACTOR: MORGAN ASHURST
CONTRACT VALUE: £2,450,000
DATE OF COMPLETION: FEBRUARY 2009
GROSS INTERNAL AREA: 1330 SQ. M
IMAGES: WAYNE BENNETT (RIGHT); DAN TALKES (LEFT)

The Hyde is a residential adult-education centre in the grounds
of Grade II*-listed Dillington House. The studios are housed in a
black-stained cedar-clad box that seems to float over a lower level
and cantilevers out over the landscape and historic garden walls.
In the lower level, which is glazed on two sides, are dining rooms.
A long, low, grass-roofed residential block contains en suite
accommodation, with each room having a small private terrace.

The building displays a spatial and formal sophistication, a
precision and a quiet confidence that are incredibly rare. It sits with
real sensitivity within a very complex site, mediating changes in
level, capturing light and framing views. It is a fabulous addition
to the fine collection of historic buildings that exist on the site.

Section

REDNOCK SCHOOL
KINGSHILL ROAD, DURSLEY, GLOUCESTERSHIRE

CUBE DESIGN

CLIENTS: REDNOCK SCHOOL; GLOUCESTERSHIRE COUNTY COUNCIL
STRUCTURAL ENGINEER: HYDER CONSULTING
SERVICES ENGINEER: JONES KING
CONTRACTOR: SIR ROBERT MCALPINE
CONTRACT VALUE: £28,000,000
DATE OF COMPLETION: SEPTEMBER 2009
GROSS INTERNAL AREA: 11,239 SQ. M
IMAGES: CUBE DESIGN (TOP); SRM (BOTTOM)
SHORTLISTED FOR THE RIBA SORRELL FOUNDATION SCHOOLS AWARD

Rednock School, a BSF (Building Schools for the Future) Pathfinder school for 1450 pupils, is a three-storey building occupying two wings cranked in plan, each organized around a generous linear atrium/circulation space that runs the height and length of the building, and each top-lit by an ETFE roof. At intervals the atrium broadens into open seating areas and quirky pod-like break-out spaces. Classrooms are set either side of the atrium, and have views over landscaped gardens and the countryside beyond.

The generosity, openness and lightness of the building are uplifting, and contribute to its easy and relaxed operation. Rednock School has one of the highest BREEAM 'Excellent' ratings for an educational building in the country.

First-floor plan

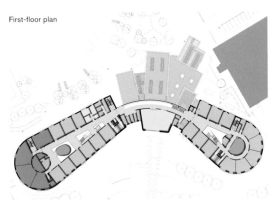

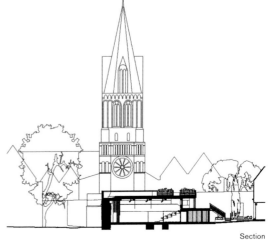

CORPUS CHRISTI COLLEGE AUDITORIUM
MERTON STREET, OXFORD

RICK MATHER ARCHITECTS

CLIENT: CORPUS CHRISTI COLLEGE
STRUCTURAL ENGINEER: ENGINEERS HASKINS ROBINSON WATERS
SERVICES ENGINEER: MOTT MACDONALD
CONTRACTOR: BEARD
CONTRACT VALUE: £2,100,000
DATE OF COMPLETION: JUNE 2009
GROSS INTERNAL AREA: 360 SQ. M
IMAGES: RICK MATHER ARCHITECTS
SHORTLISTED FOR THE CROWN ESTATE CONSERVATION AWARD

This scheme, won in an invited RIBA competition, sets the desire to provide a new multi-purpose performance space against the need to retain precious open space. The solution is both ingenious and simple: to occupy a corner enclosed by a thirteenth-century city wall and one of its bastions, burying the auditorium within these structures and wrapping new gardens over the top.

The site is within a scheduled ancient monument, a registered garden, a conservation area and a site of great archaeological importance, while the adjoining college buildings are all Grade I-listed. Within such an onerous set of constraints, the resultant building is both an essay in conservation and a work of great clarity and invention.

Section

THE GATEWAY, BUCKINGHAMSHIRE NEW UNIVERSITY
QUEEN ALEXANDRA ROAD, HIGH WYCOMBE

RMJM

CLIENT: THE GATEWAY, BUCKINGHAMSHIRE NEW UNIVERSITY
STRUCTURAL ENGINEER: AECOM
SERVICES ENGINEER: MOTT MACDONALD
CONTRACTOR: BAM
CONTRACT VALUE: £27,000,000
DATE OF COMPLETION: SEPTEMBER 2009
GROSS INTERNAL AREA: 10,578 SQ. M
IMAGES: HUFTON + CROW – VIEW

The building occupies a prominent, roughly triangular site adjacent to a quadruple roundabout, and by its siting creates a new public space for the town. It provides a wide range of 24/7 facilities, including a sports hall, a learning resource centre, a dance studio, a gym, and video and drama studios – a seemingly impossible mix of uses that have been magically squeezed into a muscular and writhing form.

Externally, to contain this box of tricks, the six-storey faceted building is clad in a stainless-steel material with a surface that produces colour through a refractory process, so that as the light changes it creates an iridescence of greens, violets and blues reminiscent of tropical fish – completing a truly spectacular gateway to the university and the town.

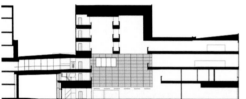

Section

WATER HALL PRIMARY SCHOOL
FERN GROVE, BLETCHLEY

ARCHITECTURE MK (NOW CLOSED), MILTON KEYNES
COUNCIL

CLIENT: MILTON KEYNES COUNCIL
STRUCTURAL ENGINEER: ADAMS KARA TAYLOR
SERVICES ENGINEERS: ARCHITECTURE MK;
      MILTON KEYNES COUNCIL
CONTRACTOR: DEEJAK
CONTRACT VALUE: £5,227,000
DATE OF COMPLETION: OCTOBER 2008
GROSS INTERNAL AREA: 2450 SQ. M
IMAGES: REDSHIFT

The school is set in an area of high unemployment and social problems, and it has a strong ethos that seeks to provide a haven for its children. The head teacher says that 'people did not want an intimidating building, but a place with a soul'.

Water Hall is a friendly jumble of forms and materials. A brick-framed moon gate opens into a conventional lobby, but through a glazed screen a large internal courtyard is glimpsed and the world turns topsy-turvy. This is an informal space of great variety, and one that is exuberant and very pleasurable.

The building is bursting with ideas. It avoids normal educational and architectural credos, producing a design that calms young minds in order to allow learning while simultaneously delighting them.

Sectional elevation

WELCH HOUSE
GURNARD, ISLE OF WIGHT

THE MANSER PRACTICE

CLIENTS: MR AND MRS WELCH
STRUCTURAL ENGINEER: ELLIOTT WOOD PARTNERSHIP
CONTRACTOR: JOHN PECK CONSTRUCTION
CONTRACT VALUE: £500,000
DATE OF COMPLETION: JANUARY 2009
GROSS INTERNAL AREA: 244 SQ. M
IMAGES: MORLEY VON STERNBERG – ARCAID

Occupying a sloping wooded foreshore, the house sits as a shiny black box hovering above the slope and is accessed by a small bridge. From the entrance, a beautifully crafted concrete spiral staircase leads to an open living space with breathtaking views across the Solent. Downstairs are bedrooms and bathrooms, all simply laid out and elegant.

The house has a very matter-of-fact quality to it that picks up on the craft of boatbuilding. And as the sunset transforms the Fawley oil refinery on the other side of the Solent, the famous image of Pierre Koenig's Case Study House No. 22 of 1960, with the lights of Los Angeles glittering away beyond to the horizon, is brought to mind – quite an achievement on the Isle of Wight.

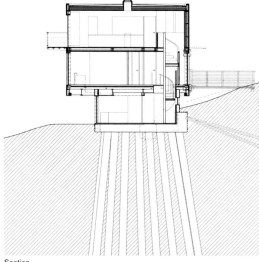

Section

WELLSTEAD PRIMARY SCHOOL
WELLSTEAD WAY, HEDGE END, HAMPSHIRE

HAMPSHIRE COUNTY COUNCIL

CLIENTS: HAMPSHIRE COUNTY COUNCIL CHILDREN'S SERVICES; RICHARD
    WHARTON (HEAD TEACHER)
STRUCTURAL ENGINEER: PRICE & MYERS
SERVICES ENGINEERS: RHB PARTNERSHIP; HAMPSHIRE COUNTY COUNCIL
    PROPERTY SERVICES
CONTRACTOR: BAM
CONTRACT VALUE: £4,376,000
DATE OF COMPLETION: SEPTEMBER 2008
GROSS INTERNAL AREA: 1420 SQ. M
IMAGES: DAN KEELER

A one-form entry primary serving 210 children, Wellstead is set within the Dowd's Farm housing development in a Tudorbethan suburb of Southampton. What sets it apart straight away is its absolute clarity. One arrives to views through a low, glazed library space to a courtyard and playground, which is set between two taller pitched-roof forms that contain classrooms. This clarity is founded on a collegiate typology that goes back to the monasteries that prefigured schools and colleges – an educational paradigm.

Recognizably a 'Hampshire school' that continues the legacy of Sir Colin Stansfield Smith's imprint on school design in the 1970s and 1980s, this building makes the difficult look simple, and creates a school that could act as a blueprint for any educational project.

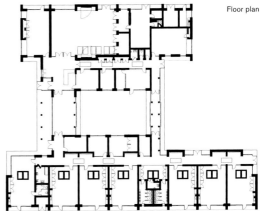

Floor plan

WOOTTON PLACE
WOOTTON, OXFORDSHIRE

YIANGOU ARCHITECTS

CLIENT: PRIVATE
STRUCTURAL ENGINEER: GIFFORD
SERVICES ENGINEER: CBG CONSULTANTS
CONTRACTOR: SYMM AND COMPANY
CONTRACT VALUE: £7,000,000
DATE OF COMPLETION: JUNE 2009
GROSS INTERNAL AREA: 2000 SQ. M
IMAGES: ED KINGSFORD PHOTOGRAPHY

The complete conservation and renovation of Wootton Place, a Georgian country house in the Cotswolds, have been perfectly well realized by the architect, but what really is exceptional is the new swimming-pool pavilion in the walled garden.

In fact, the pavilion consists almost solely of a floating roof: the walls are fully glazed sliding screens that retract to open up the pool space to the garden, while the roof sits on a perimeter grid of dark steel columns. A large rooflight running the length of the pool slides open, so that the roof becomes reduced to a frame for the sky. This beautiful floating – almost vanishing – building has a wonderful, ephemeral quality that is rare in architecture.

Ground-floor plan

CRAWLEY LIBRARY
SOUTHGATE AVENUE, CRAWLEY

PENOYRE & PRASAD

CLIENT: WEST SUSSEX COUNTY COUNCIL
LANDSCAPE ARCHITECT: LIZARD LANDSCAPE DESIGN
STRUCTURAL/SERVICES ENGINEER: GIFFORD
QUANTITY SURVEYOR: CURRIE & BROWN
PROJECT MANAGER: MACE
ACOUSTICS CONSULTANT: APPLIED ACOUSTIC DESIGN
ARTS CONSULTANT: GINKGO PROJECTS
FIRE CONSULTANT: BURO HAPPOLD FEDRA
CONTRACTOR: BAM
CONTRACT VALUE: £12,564,136
DATE OF OCCUPATION: DECEMBER 2008
GROSS INTERNAL AREA: 4470 SQ. M
IMAGES: TIMOTHY SOAR

This very civic scheme has a strong and dignified presence, and reinvents the spirit of the new town. The design-and-build project sets an admirably high benchmark of quality, with well-considered form, massing and articulation of all the façades. Inside, it becomes evident how hard the building is working; it has three distinct uses – library, registry and social services – yet it accommodates these distinct public activities with apparent architectural ease.

There is plenty of natural daylight within a deep plan, and a generous timber staircase works well with the carved artwork tree trunks dotted around the library floors. The sustainability credentials are good, with a biomass boiler (using local woodchips), solar heating and green roofs.

Section

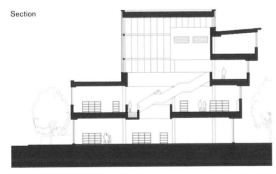

Section

MILL HOUSE
MILL HOUSE FARM, ASHFORD, KENT

CTM ARCHITECTS (NOW GUY HOLLAWAY ARCHITECTS)

CLIENT: PRIVATE
LANDSCAPE ARCHITECT: IAIN MACDONALD DESIGN
STRUCTURAL ENGINEER: A.J. LOCKE CONSULTING ENGINEERS
SERVICES ENGINEER: DIXON DEBOISE
CONTRACTOR: COOMBS (CANTERBURY)
CONTRACT VALUE: CONFIDENTIAL
DATE OF OCCUPATION: JANUARY 2010
GROSS INTERNAL AREA: 531 SQ. M
IMAGES: PAUL FREEMAN

To say that this project involved simply the adaptation of an old Georgian mill house and the creation of a new modernist extension fails to do justice to the ambition of the scheme. A controlled, creative dialogue between the architect and client has resulted in a home that not only is beautifully crafted, but also cleverly exploits given conditions of levels, key views and ancient fabric to concoct a sequence of spaces that feels very natural.

The natural conditions are exploited for energy: ground-source hot water from under the lawn and solar panels on the roof. Sustainability is further enhanced by the new extension's sedum roofs, which are elegantly trimmed with zinc.

SCHOOL OF ARTS
UNIVERSITY OF KENT, CANTERBURY

HAWKINS\BROWN

CLIENT: UNIVERSITY OF KENT
LANDSCAPE ARCHITECT: FARRER HUXLEY ASSOCIATES
STRUCTURAL SERVICES AND ACOUSTICS ENGINEER: ARUP
QUANTITY SURVEYOR: NORTHCROFT
PLANNING CONSULTANT: CMA PLANNING
CONTRACTOR: MORGAN ASHURST
CONTRACT VALUE: £6,000,000
DATE OF OCCUPATION: 18 JANUARY 2010
GROSS INTERNAL AREA: 2510 SQ. M
IMAGES: DANIEL CLEMENTS – VIEW

The School of Arts succeeds in terms of both its architectural presence on the university campus and its interiors, which reinforce a sense of community in teachers and students. Both of these groups benefit from well-delivered studios for drama, film and visual arts.

Above the perimeter, accessible and well-lit clusters of staff offices surround the heart of the school: a three-storey open atrium, which has tough finishes of steel and timber to the balustrades. A simple internal colour palette of red, black, white and grey has been adopted, while externally zinc shingle sheets predominate as a self-finished cladding that should continue to look good over time. This building demonstrates how successful design can improve learning, and is an exemplar for future campus architecture.

Section

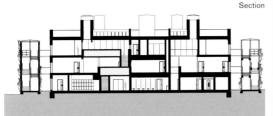

TOWNER
DEVONSHIRE PARK, COLLEGE ROAD, EASTBOURNE

RICK MATHER ARCHITECTS

CLIENT: EASTBOURNE BOROUGH COUNCIL
STRUCTURAL ENGINEER: DEWHURST MACFARLANE & PARTNERS
SERVICES ENGINEER: MOTT MACDONALD
ACOUSTICS CONSULTANT: SANDY BROWN ASSOCIATES
LIGHTING CONSULTANT: DPA LIGHTING CONSULTANTS
COST CONSULTANT: GARDINER & THEOBALD
CONTRACTOR: MORGAN ASHURST
CONTRACT VALUE: £8,600,000
DATE OF OCCUPATION: JANUARY 2009
GROSS INTERNAL AREA: 2600 SQ. M
IMAGES: JAMES BRITTAIN – VIEW (BOTTOM LEFT); DANIEL CLEMENTS – VIEW
    (BOTTOM RIGHT); DAVID WATSON (TOP)

This beautiful and resourceful building houses some stunning concrete-shell gallery spaces, and it achieves a remarkable feat of connecting well both visually and physically with the classic–modernist conference centre next door. As well as the seemingly limitless range of activities it can accommodate, it houses the remarkable Towner art collection, which is kept in very accessible but well-managed conditions.

Spatially, the building is easy to read, and it focuses on some key views of the South Downs by the use of large areas of glazing, particularly from the cafe at the top. The entrance atrium and stairs feel spacious for what is a compact building, and this feeling is enhanced by the clever use of the transverse slot through the building at all the key levels.

Site plan

1–5 BATEMAN MEWS
SW4

ANNE THORNE ARCHITECTS PARTNERSHIP

CLIENT: METROPOLITAN HOUSING PARTNERSHIP
STRUCTURAL ENGINEER: TARGET TIMBER SYSTEMS
CONTRACTOR: BONDS BUILDERS & CONTRACTORS
CONTRACT VALUE: £900,000
DATE OF COMPLETION: JUNE 2009
GROSS INTERNAL AREA: 532 SQ. M
IMAGES: IOANA MARINESCU
SHORTLISTED FOR THE STEPHEN LAWRENCE PRIZE

Every now and again one experiences a scheme, such as Bateman Mews, that contains a tangible sense of humanity: not 'big' architecture, but sensitive, inspiring and uplifting design that positively affects the lives of people who use it.

The houses are essentially two-storey dwellings, but through the clever use of the staircase half-landings, a lower and an upper mezzanine have been created, providing two extra bedrooms in addition to the two bedrooms in the main body of the house. The most intriguing aspects of the scheme are the use of timber shingles as cladding and the articulation of the section and massing to create upturned eaves and setbacks. Both of these features are extremely attractive and create a distinct sense of *rus in urbe*.

Typical house plans

Plan

7 JULY MEMORIAL
HYDE PARK, W1

CARMODY GROARKE

CLIENT: THE ROYAL PARKS
LANDSCAPE ARCHITECT: COLVIN & MOGGRIDGE
STRUCTURAL ENGINEER: ARUP
CONTRACTOR: WALTER LILLY
CONTRACT VALUE: £600,000
DATE OF COMPLETION: JULY 2009
GROSS INTERNAL AREA: 250 SQ. M
IMAGES: GAUTIER DEBLONDE
SHORTLISTED FOR THE RIBA CABE PUBLIC SPACE AWARD AND THE STEPHEN
    LAWRENCE PRIZE
THE ROYAL PARKS WAS SHORTLISTED FOR THE RIBA CLIENT OF THE YEAR

The architect took a highly collaborative approach, involving the bereaved families throughout the design process. It has succeeded in articulating in abstract form a manifestation of the singular and the personal, the collective and the civic. The four 'rooms' of the memorial acknowledge the four events of 7 July 2005 and the four communities of loss.

The choice of material is also highly successful. The fifty-two cast stainless-steel stelae appear at first glance to be identical, but they are in fact all different. They have a sense of permanence, solemnity and solidity, but on closer inspection the fluidity of the moment of pouring is visible, providing a subtle reference to the moment of rupture of the explosions that caused the tragedy.

60 THREADNEEDLE STREET
EC2

ERIC PARRY ARCHITECTS

CLIENT: HAMMERSON
STRUCTURAL ENGINEER: WSP CANTOR SEINUK
SERVICES ENGINEER: HILSON MORAN
FAÇADE ENGINEER: ARUP
CONTRACTOR: BOVIS LEND LEASE
CONTRACT VALUE: £64,000,000
DATE OF COMPLETION: JANUARY 2009
GROSS INTERNAL AREA: 28,811 SQ. M
IMAGES: TIMOTHY SOAR
HAMMERSON WAS WINNER OF THE RIBA CLIENT OF THE YEAR

The brief for a new speculative office building in the City originated from an inauspicious existing footprint. The architect has pushed the limits of site, envelope and cost to create a building that responds to both the street pattern and the neighbouring masterpiece – Sir John Soane's Bank of England.

The three façades are urbane and sophisticated in character, a dark, textured layering of transoms and mullions, with coloured- and curved-glass elements. The deep plan is offset by a generous gallery foyer that draws the visitor to a beautiful light-well at the centre, and on to leather-clad lifts.

This building raises the game for speculative office design, demonstrating that design-orientated architects can bring much greater value to the City than mere profit.

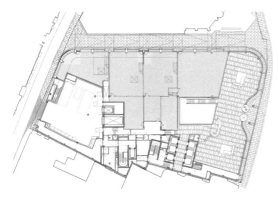

Ground-floor plan

BANKSIDE 123
SOUTHWARK STREET, SE1

ALLIES AND MORRISON ARCHITECTS

CLIENT: LAND SECURITIES
STRUCTURAL ENGINEER: RAMBOLL UK
SERVICES ENGINEER: FOREMAN ROBERTS
CONTRACTOR: BOVIS LEND LEASE
CONTRACT VALUE: CONFIDENTIAL
DATE OF COMPLETION: 2009
GROSS INTERNAL AREA: 119,450 SQ. M
IMAGES: DENNIS GILBERT – VIEW (BOTTOM RIGHT); IPC MEDIA/
    HUFTON + CROW – VIEW (TOP; BOTTOM LEFT)

This project is a large commercial development immediately behind
Tate Modern on Southwark Street. Building 1 is much the best of
the three buildings (the other two were fitted out by the client). It is
known as the Blue Fin owing to the 2000 blue aluminium fins on the
façade. The fins work like leaves on trees, providing dappled solar
shading without taking out too much indirect light, and breaking up
the façade. The internal spaces are arranged around a dramatic
central atrium with a series of open bridges crossing at each floor
level, making the movement of people around the building clearly
visible. For such a large building, it is well mannered and provides
a high benchmark for commercial architecture.

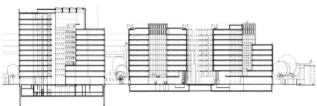

Section

BUS DRIVER FACILITY
CHEQUERS LANE, DAGENHAM

JULIAN COWIE ARCHITECTS

CLIENT: TRANSPORT FOR LONDON
STRUCTURAL/SERVICES ENGINEER: PARSONS BRINCKERHOFF
CONTRACTOR: SKANSKA INFRASTRUCTURE SERVICES
CONTRACT VALUE: £210,000
DATE OF COMPLETION: JANUARY 2010
GROSS INTERNAL AREA: 61 SQ. M
IMAGES: TIM CROCKER
SHORTLISTED FOR THE STEPHEN LAWRENCE PRIZE

Bus drivers, pausing for a break at the end of their route, are welcomed by this enigmatic little building, set within a carefully considered hard landscape. The building is not only somewhere to have a drink and use the toilet; it is also a new marker for travellers in a post-industrial wilderness, and a symbol of what is to come.

The most intriguing aspect of the building is the contrast between a plain exterior of tough, perforated stainless steel and the high specification and use of colour in the interior. This pioneer facility creates a powerful presence, contributing to rather than being dwarfed by the A13 flyover overhead. Civilizing an industrial wasteland awaiting regeneration, the building is architecture's David to the highway's Goliath.

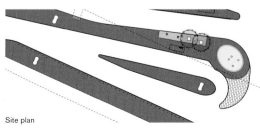

Site plan

CHARLOTTE BUILDING
GRESSE STREET, W1

LIFSCHUTZ DAVIDSON SANDILANDS

CLIENT: DERWENT LONDON
STRUCTURAL ENGINEER: ADAMS KARA TAYLOR
SERVICES ENGINEER: NORMAN DISNEY & YOUNG
CONTRACTOR: BALFOUR BEATTY CONSTRUCTION SCOTTISH & SOUTHERN
CONTRACT VALUE: CONFIDENTIAL
DATE OF COMPLETION: NOVEMBER 2009
GROSS INTERNAL AREA: 6088 SQ. M
IMAGES: CHRIS GASCOIGNE – VIEW
LONGLISTED FOR THE RIBA STIRLING PRIZE

This highly accomplished speculative office project is the result of collaboration between an experienced client committed to design quality and an architect with years of experience refining this building typology. The project, which appears to reference the Daily Express Building on Fleet Street, brings the design firmly into the twenty-first century and turns a relatively small backlands site into a substantial addition to the West End streetscape.

The design solution combines good-quality materials and detailing with a sophisticated and sustainable environmental strategy. The bespoke cladding subtly maximizes natural light while controlling solar gain; the project has opening windows and secure night-time ventilation to allow cooling of the exposed-concrete ceilings. The building appears to be a success because it is already fully let, just months after completion.

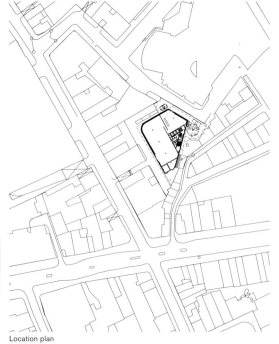

Location plan

COLLEGE ROAD
SE21

KNOX BHAVAN ARCHITECTS

CLIENTS: TOM AND BRENDA WELLS
LANDSCAPE DESIGNER: DAN PEARSON STUDIO
STRUCTURAL ENGINEER: ELLIOTT WOOD PARTNERSHIP
SERVICES ENGINEER: MENDICK WARING
CONTRACTOR: R. DURTNELL & SONS
CONTRACT VALUE: CONFIDENTIAL
DATE OF COMPLETION: JULY 2009
GROSS INTERNAL AREA: 580 SQ. M
IMAGES: RICHARD HAUGHTON

College Road is an exceptional one-off family house. While being contemporary, it clearly continues the Arts and Crafts tradition without being derivative. There is real invention in the form and in the detail and material execution. The architect has managed to accommodate all the demands of a family of six and to create a tangible sense of place. This is definitely a home as well as a piece of architecture.

The functional programme is clearly expressed in the built form, particularly through the use of the curved walls, the glass roof lanterns over the bathrooms and the glass canopy and lenses adjacent to the garden. The material juxtaposition of craft-based masonry and oak with minimally detailed glass elements is especially pleasing.

Ground-floor plan

EDWARD ALLEYN BUILDING
ALLEYN'S SCHOOL, TOWNLEY ROAD, SE22

VAN HEYNINGEN AND HAWARD ARCHITECTS

CLIENT: ALLEYN'S SCHOOL
STRUCTURAL ENGINEER: PRICE & MYERS
SERVICES ENGINEER: MAX FORDHAM
CONTRACTOR: ROOFF
CONTRACT VALUE: £8,400,000
DATE OF COMPLETION: AUGUST 2008
GROSS INTERNAL AREA: 3510 SQ. M
IMAGES: NICK KANE – ARCAID

Rather than continue with its previous piecemeal expansion, the school took a good look at what it really needed. The building contains the Michael Croft Theatre and provides a link back to the National Youth Theatre, which developed out of the school in the 1960s. Additionally, it provides a sixth-form study centre, an IT suite, a careers facility, bases for various teaching departments and a 100-seat lecture theatre. The building is deep in plan, but does not look bulky in reality. Other accommodation is in the form of glass boxes, which help to break down the mass and give it animation.

The project stands as a beacon of quality in the midst of some rather bland accommodation. Every school should have a building such as this.

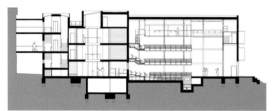

Section

FOREST OF LIGHT
W1

TONKIN LIU

CLIENTS: JILL ROACH AND JOHN BROOME
STRUCTURAL ENGINEER: PRICE & MYERS
SERVICES ENGINEER: ARCHINEERS
CONTRACTOR: ROACH AND PARTNERS
CONTRACT VALUE: CONFIDENTIAL
DATE OF COMPLETION: APRIL 2008
GROSS INTERNAL AREA: 265 SQ. M
IMAGES: SUE BARR – VIEW

The architect has transformed an awkward, L-shaped attic space
that had lain derelict for fifty years into a calm oasis high above the
roofs of Marylebone. The two former maid's quarters atop a Grade
II-listed Beaux Art residential building have been joined and fitted
out as timber-panelled rooms in bleached oak-veneered panels.

The project is an exercise in the play of light, sky and the
colour white. White powder-coated aluminium panels with a
perforated tree motif are the design focus of the scheme. They
are used to moderate the ventilation, the heating, the light around
the windows and the oversized rooflights. The well-resolved
relationship between inside and out allows the client to derive
maximum benefit from the extraordinary location.

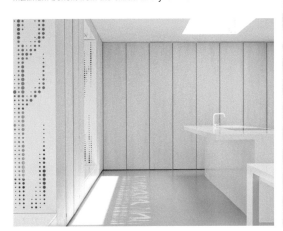

THE FORGE/CAPONATA
DELANCEY STREET, NW1

BURD HAWARD ARCHITECTS

CLIENT: CALYX PROPERTY
STRUCTURAL ENGINEER: ARUP
SERVICES ENGINEER: MAX FORDHAM
CONTRACTOR: CRISPIN & BORST
CONTRACT VALUE: CONFIDENTIAL
DATE OF COMPLETION: MAY 2009
GROSS INTERNAL AREA: 735 SQ. M
IMAGES: HÉLÈNE BINET

This intricate mixed-use development is one of a number of RIBA Award-winning schemes this year that demonstrate the creativity of architects and their ability to respond to complex and sometimes contradictory briefs. It includes a 125-seat recital hall, which has to be acoustically suitable for both live performance and recording; a cafe/bar and restaurant; and three studio flats.

The family who developed and now run the small complex include classically trained musicians and a restaurateur. The recital hall and the cafe/restaurant/flats are accommodated in two separate brick-clad volumes, connected by a double-height glazed-in courtyard space, letting daylight and natural ventilation into the heart of the plan and allowing the public parts of the building to be used independently or as a single space.

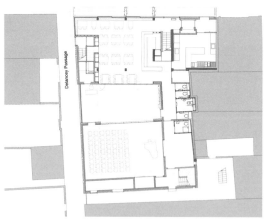

Ground-floor plan

HIGHBURY SQUARE
N5

ALLIES AND MORRISON ARCHITECTS

CLIENT: HIGHBURY HOLDINGS
STRUCTURAL ENGINEER: BURO HAPPOLD
SERVICES ENGINEER: HOARE LEA
CONTRACTOR: SIR ROBERT MCALPINE
CONTRACT VALUE: £170,000,000
DATE OF COMPLETION: JULY 2009
IMAGES: DENNIS GILBERT – VIEW
LONGLISTED FOR THE RIBA STIRLING PRIZE

The challenging and almost implausible brief called for the conversion of the former Arsenal football ground into 700 new dwellings as part of a new residential neighbourhood while retaining the listed East Stand and the West Stand. The key move was to keep the pitch area as the open space of the new development and to mirror the scale of the former stands in the new, highly successful north and south blocks.

The new square, which can be entered at each of the corners, has become the focus of the development. The project has created a unique new living space for London. It is surprisingly effective in maintaining the memory of the previous use without compromising the new domestic environment.

Section

LEAF HOUSE
NW3

JAMES GORST ARCHITECTS

CLIENT: PRIVATE
STRUCTURAL ENGINEER: ALAN BAXTER & ASSOCIATES
SERVICES ENGINEER: CHAPMAN BATHURST
CONTRACTOR: R. DURTNELL & SONS
CONTRACT VALUE: £2,650,000
DATE OF COMPLETION: DECEMBER 2008
GROSS INTERNAL AREA: 575 SQ. M
IMAGES: HÉLÈNE BINET
SHORTLISTED FOR THE RIBA MANSER MEDAL

This is a thoughtful contemporary interpretation of a traditional large London town house. The rooms are tailored to fulfil the needs of a family with two growing children and two parents who work from home. There is one study in the pavilion on the roof and another in the basement, lit by a large glass light flush with the pavement.

Although this is a big house, it is extremely well judged and varied in its detail, and its concerns are those of so many smaller family homes. Acoustic separation of spaces was key to the brief, and there are many neat features, such as doors that can close off otherwise open-plan arrangements into separate spaces. Overall simplicity is overlaid with richness of detail.

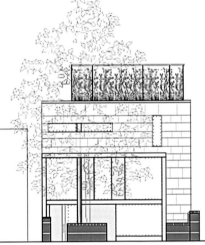

Elevation

LONGFORD COMMUNITY SCHOOL LIBRARY
TACHBROOK ROAD, FELTHAM

JONATHAN CLARK ARCHITECTS

CLIENT: LONGFORD COMMUNITY SCHOOL
STRUCTURAL ENGINEER: FLUID STRUCTURES
SERVICES ENGINEER: BHP MECHANICAL
CONTRACTOR: HORGAN BROS
CONTRACT VALUE: £1,115,000
DATE OF COMPLETION: SEPTEMBER 2009
GROSS INTERNAL AREA: 750 SQ. M
IMAGES: PETER COOK – VIEW

This project is an exemplar of how more can be achieved for less. A modest budget and a 5-metre extension added to a mundane, dilapidated 1960s block have transformed the whole into an exciting new addition both externally and internally, the impact of which far exceeds its size and cost.

The colourful Finnforest structural fins create a bold articulated elevation and also provide environmental protection. Internally, the library, with its bespoke, architect-designed furniture, has clearly produced a flexible and stimulating learning space; even the carpet cubes double as props in maths lessons. The organically shaped auditorium is also a highly successful intervention. It has a special feel, yet that has been achieved through simple, careful detailing.

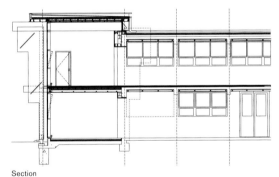

Section

LOWTHER CHILDREN'S CENTRE
STILLINGFLEET ROAD, SW13

PATEL TAYLOR

CLIENT: LONDON BOROUGH OF RICHMOND UPON THAMES
STRUCTURAL ENGINEER: CONISBEE
SERVICES ENGINEER: MICHAEL POPPER ASSOCIATES
CONTRACTOR: LAKEHOUSE
CONTRACT VALUE: £1,400,000
DATE OF COMPLETION: SEPTEMBER 2009
GROSS INTERNAL AREA: 590 SQ. M
IMAGES: CHARLOTTE WOOD – ARCAID
SHORTLISTED FOR THE RIBA SORRELL FOUNDATION SCHOOLS AWARD

This imaginative and inventive project involves a modest, unashamedly contemporary addition to an existing school, providing it with a new entrance and a whole new identity. The impact of the addition belies its size. The fluid yet clear plan responds effortlessly to its context, creating a light-filled central circulation spine from which the learning and support spaces are accessed.

As much creative thought has been lavished on the fittings as on the form and fabric of the building. For example, the linear, sloping storage wall that divides two reception spaces creates child-sized hideaways, playhouses and shops, and extends into the playground to become the play equipment. The result is a highly consistent, charming and ingenious whole.

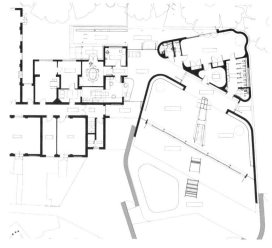

Ground-floor plan

MEDIEVAL & RENAISSANCE GALLERIES
VICTORIA AND ALBERT MUSEUM, SW7

MUMA WITH JULIAN HARRAP ARCHITECTS

CLIENT: TRUSTEES OF THE VICTORIA AND ALBERT MUSEUM
STRUCTURAL ENGINEER: DEWHURST MACFARLANE AND PARTNERS
SERVICES ENGINEER: ARUP
CONTRACTOR: HOLLOWAY WHITE ALLOM
CONTRACT VALUE: £21,500,000
DATE OF COMPLETION: DECEMBER 2009
GROSS INTERNAL AREA: 4500 SQ. M
IMAGES: ALAN WILLIAMS
LONGLISTED FOR THE RIBA STIRLING PRIZE
VICTORIA AND ALBERT MUSEUM WAS SHORTLISTED FOR THE RIBA CLIENT
    OF THE YEAR

This project is a joy from beginning to end, and represents a brave commission from a practice that was then only three years old. The design is part newbuild, part archaeology. It is respectful to the original Aston Webb architecture without any hint of sentimentality; on closer inspection, it is even quietly radical, with major improvements to the circulation and the creation of a new glazed roof around Webb's original apsidal plan form.

Where restoration or extension of the existing fabric was required, the architect worked with Julian Harrap Architects to develop an appropriate detail, be it the extension of an existing pilaster or of an original marble staircase, creating a seamless narrative of old and new.

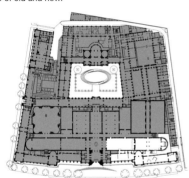

Site plan

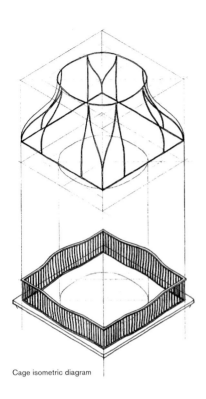

Cage isometric diagram

THE MONUMENT
EC3

JULIAN HARRAP ARCHITECTS

CLIENT: CITY OF LONDON
STRUCTURAL ENGINEER: HOCKLEY & DAWSON
SERVICES ENGINEER: SPENCER CLARKE PARTNERSHIP
CONTRACTOR: CATHEDRAL WORKS ORGANISATION (CHICHESTER)
CONTRACT VALUE: £3,200,000
DATE OF COMPLETION: FEBRUARY 2009
GROSS INTERNAL AREA: 130 SQ. M
IMAGES: SUE SALTON
SHORTLISTED FOR THE CROWN ESTATE CONSERVATION AWARD

Sir Christopher Wren's much-loved Monument to the Great Fire of London of 1666 had suffered from the relentless erosion of rain and tourism, and latterly the challenge of twenty-first-century safety regulations. The architect has made careful judgements about when to restore and when to intervene visibly and deliberately.

The major intervention of the stainless-steel viewing 'cage' was a design risk that has paid off. In conception, form and detail, it succeeds in offering far better public access, while creating a dialogue with the original host structure. It is a baroque-inspired construction of which Wren might well have approved.

Julian Harrap Architects' achievement in the restoration of the column is one not only of invisible conservation, but also of perceptive revelation and transformation.

NEW HORIZON YOUTH CENTRE
CHALTON STREET, NW1

ADAM KHAN ARCHITECTS

CLIENT: NEW HORIZON YOUTH CENTRE
STRUCTURAL ENGINEER: PRICE & MYERS
SERVICES ENGINEER: ROBINSON ASSOCIATES
CONTRACTOR: JOHN O'NEILL & PARTNERS
CONTRACT VALUE: £1,146,896
DATE OF COMPLETION: FEBRUARY 2010
GROSS INTERNAL AREA: 620 SQ. M
IMAGES: ADAM KHAN ARCHITECTS (BOTTOM LEFT AND RIGHT);
        DAVID GRANDORGE (TOP)

The youth centre, for homeless young people, is part of a 1920s London County Council estate. From the street, the building remains largely unchanged, but the architect has added an extension to the side with a large copper roof and a dramatic dormer. The design picks up on the Art Deco details of the original structure, adding to the somewhat Central European character of the estate.

Internally, the project avoids any sense of being institutional; it is both homely and fashionable. A new cantilever stair works gracefully within the constraints of modern stair regulations, and looks as if it has always been there.

The great achievement of this project lies in the individual care and consideration that have been given to each of the spaces, and in the details, which are always warm and welcoming.

Elevation

NORTHBURY INFANT AND JUNIOR SCHOOL
NORTH STREET, BARKING

GREENHILL JENNER

CLIENT: LONDON BOROUGH OF BARKING & DAGENHAM
STRUCTURAL/SERVICES ENGINEER: BWM
CONTRACTOR: NEILCOTT CONSTRUCTION
CONTRACT VALUE: £4,500,000
DATE OF COMPLETION: MARCH 2009
GROSS INTERNAL AREA: 1967 SQ. M
IMAGES: CHARLOTTE WOOD – ARCAID

The project provides a new classroom block and façade to a large Victorian brick school. With its big windows and high ceilings, the old building was deliberately retained as an important historical example of belief in education and as part of the overall sustainability strategy.

The architect has created a relaxed, airy and warm atmosphere with the timber-and-glass construction, which takes its cue from the spatial generosity and proportions of the old building, and matches it with a humane intimacy not often found in contemporary state-sector architecture.

The insulated coloured-glass front façade, with its reflective relation to existing trees, succeeds in superimposing an elegant statement about the twenty-first-century commitment to education on the grim nineteenth-century institutional composition.

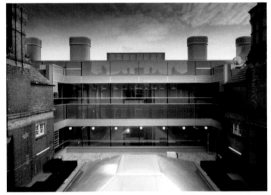

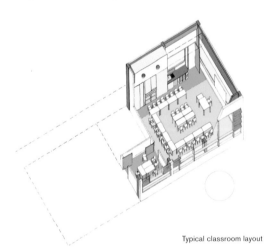

Typical classroom layout

PARK AVENUE SOUTH
N8

STUDIO OCTOPI

CLIENT: PRIVATE
STRUCTURAL ENGINEER: PRICE & MYERS
CONTRACTOR: FAMELLA BUILDING CONTRACTORS
CONTRACT VALUE: £246,000
DATE OF COMPLETION: SEPTEMBER 2009
GROSS INTERNAL AREA: 93.5 SQ. M
IMAGES: LYNDON DOUGLAS

This major extension to a late Victorian end-of-terrace house ties together the principal living spaces of the house, while creating a complete and enjoyable contrast. Internally, triangular white planes and similar glass sheets define the roof beyond the envelope of the existing house. The whiteness of this light and playful space is completed with a lined ash floor.

The extension is a beautifully detailed space that makes a really convincing large kitchen/dining room within an extension of limited size. The lighting is well integrated within the edges of the rooflight, and there are two connections to the garden, one via a pivoting section of wall. From the garden the extension is a distinct geometric form, clad in standing-seam metal.

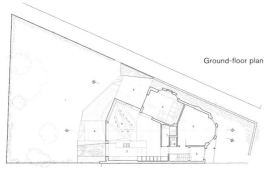

Ground-floor plan

PRIMARY SUBSTATION
OLYMPIC PARK, E15

NORD

CLIENT: EDF ENERGY
STRUCTURAL ENGINEER: ANDREWS ASSOCIATES
SERVICES ENGINEER: APPLIED ENERGY
CONTRACTOR: KIER LONDON
CONTRACT VALUE: £8,500,000
DATE OF COMPLETION: JANUARY 2010
GROSS INTERNAL AREA: 1810 SQ. M
IMAGES: ANDREW LEE (TOP; BOTTOM LEFT); OLYMPIC DELIVERY AUTHORITY
    (BOTTOM RIGHT)
LONGLISTED FOR THE RIBA STIRLING PRIZE

The Primary Substation scheme rises far beyond the mere encasing of a pair of large transformers in brick boxes. This building type is normally procured outside the profession, resulting in anonymous engineering architecture of no particular merit other than that it functions and is explosion-proof. This re-examination of the idiom, however, is an exceptional example in its rich purity, and an important contribution to the London 2012 Olympic Park environs.

The architect developed a brief for a team comprising client, engineer, architect and contractor – one that was prepared to go the distance necessary to make a lasting local monument to the Olympic Games. The close collaboration has produced a thoroughbred, a beautifully detailed and executed scheme in which function becomes sculptural landmark. The result is a convincing celebration of energy infrastructure.

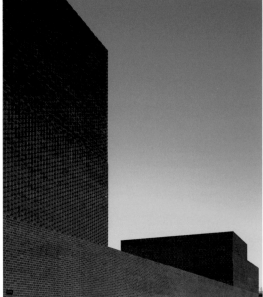

Section

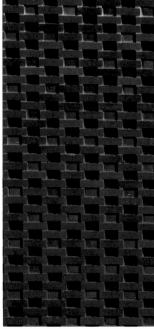

REGENT'S PLACE PAVILION
NW1

CARMODY GROARKE

CLIENT: BRITISH LAND
STRUCTURAL/SERVICES ENGINEER: ARUP
CONTRACTOR: BOVIS LEND LEASE
CONTRACT VALUE: £600,000
DATE OF COMPLETION: NOVEMBER 2009
GROSS INTERNAL AREA: 250 SQ. M
IMAGES: GAUTIER DEBLONDE
SHORTLISTED FOR THE RIBA CABE PUBLIC SPACE AWARD

This project is the realization of a competition organized by the Architecture Foundation and British Land. The completed structure is every bit as striking and simple as the concept model, successfully reflecting the height of the colonnades on the adjoining office buildings and lending the pavilion a strong connection to the site and the scale of the space. The exceptionally slender proportions of the columns and their somewhat forest-like changes in density – sometimes transparent, sometimes solid – create a beautiful moiré effect.

It is at dusk, however, that the pavilion comes into its own, filling the space with a warm light that appears to transform the cool stainless steel back into the brass of the concept model. The structure literally appears to hold the light.

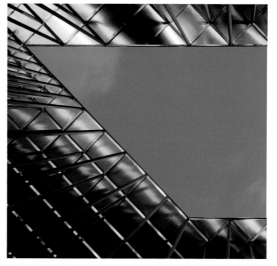

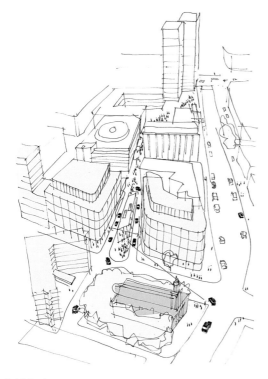

Aerial sketch

SACKLER BUILDING
HOWIE STREET, SW11

HAWORTH TOMPKINS

CLIENT: ROYAL COLLEGE OF ART
STRUCTURAL ENGINEER: PRICE & MYERS
SERVICES ENGINEER: MAX FORDHAM
CONTRACTOR: LIFE BUILD SOLUTIONS
CONTRACT VALUE: £2,900,000
DATE OF COMPLETION: OCTOBER 2009
GROSS INTERNAL AREA: 1320 SQ. M
IMAGES: HÉLÈNE BINET (TOP); PHILIP VILE (BOTTOM)

This project has taken an unremarkable industrial building and transformed it into a fine piece of contemporary architecture. The approach is clear, rational and confident. A different architect might have chosen to demolish the building and start afresh, but much would have been lost. This is not only a sustainable solution; it also maintains and enriches the character of the building and its context. This 'factory of fine art' makes a great addition to the Royal College's arts campus. The project seems to have fallen effortlessly into place once the architect discovered that the orientation of the building and the rhythm of the windows at ground level matched the brief for north light and size of studio space.

Site plan

SACKLER CENTRE FOR ARTS EDUCATION
VICTORIA AND ALBERT MUSEUM, SW7

SOFTROOM

CLIENT: VICTORIA AND ALBERT MUSEUM
STRUCTURAL/SERVICES ENGINEER: ARUP
CONTRACTOR: ALLENBUILD
CONTRACT VALUE: £3,400,000
DATE OF COMPLETION: JULY 2008
GROSS INTERNAL AREA: 1650 SQ. M
IMAGES: DENNIS GILBERT – VIEW
VICTORIA AND ALBERT MUSEUM WAS SHORTLISTED FOR THE RIBA CLIENT
     OF THE YEAR

This project impresses with the amount of amenity space provided for the museum to support its education programme, and the freshness and approach with which it was delivered. The brief called for a variety of education spaces for different age groups and constituencies, together with a flexible studio workshop for visiting designers in residence, and a fully equipped lecture theatre.

Particularly impressive is the way in which the architect has worked with the features of the existing architecture, especially the good levels of natural light and the high ceilings, and the skill with which it has fitted the new accommodation into the existing plan layout without compromising the feeling of a set of ready-made rooms. The scheme should act as an exemplar for other museums.

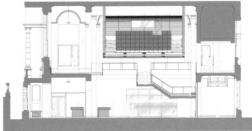

Section

TWENTY BISHOPS SQUARE/
ST BOTOLPH'S HALL
E1

MATTHEW LLOYD ARCHITECTS

CLIENTS: HAMMERSON; NATIVE LAND
STRUCTURAL ENGINEER: CLARKE NICHOLLS MARCEL
SERVICES ENGINEERS: FULLERS BUILDERS; CRISPIN & BORST;
    PAYE STONEWORK
CONTRACTOR: VINCI CONSTRUCTION UK
CONTRACT VALUE: £5,300,000
DATE OF COMPLETION: OCTOBER 2008
GROSS INTERNAL AREA: 1500 SQ. M
IMAGES: MIKAEL SCHILLING
HAMMERSON WAS WINNER OF THE RIBA CLIENT OF THE YEAR

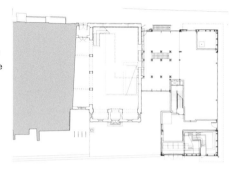

The combination of a colourful, compact new block of flats with the restoration of St Botolph's Hall has resulted in a positive, mixed-use contribution to the redevelopment of Spitalfields Market, otherwise dominated by the corporate character of retail and office.

The scheme is remarkable in its restrained composition, detailing and materiality. The admirable resolution and execution of the flats' design acknowledge the relation to the historical neighbour and create an important counterpoint to the context. With this project an interesting piece of old London has been carefully retained, and a new piece of London skilfully made.

The architect and the client have shown that, with a shrewd and strategic approach to briefing, they can create a win–win situation, addressing simultaneously the criteria for development and urban design.

Site plan

WHITECHAPEL GALLERY
WHITECHAPEL HIGH STREET, E1

ROBBRECHT EN DAEM
WITH WITHERFORD WATSON MANN ARCHITECTS

CLIENT: WHITECHAPEL GALLERY
STRUCTURAL ENGINEER: PRICE & MYERS
SERVICES ENGINEER: MAX FORDHAM
CONTRACTOR: KIER WALLIS SPECIAL PROJECTS
CONTRACT VALUE: £5,750,000
DATE OF COMPLETION: APRIL 2009
GROSS INTERNAL AREA: 3802 SQ. M
IMAGES: PETER COOK – VIEW (TOP); DAVID GRANDORGE (BOTTOM)
LONGLISTED FOR THE RIBA STIRLING PRIZE

The original gallery, by Charles Harrison Townsend, was both local and international, radical and modest. With this project, the renewed Whitechapel Gallery has demonstrated what considered architecture can do for a public institution. The collaborating architects have enhanced the existing qualities of an unpretentious, direct access to art, with particular pleasure demonstrated in skilfully connecting with the material and cultural fabric of London's East End.

The main new gallery, refreshingly not a white 'neutral' box, offers London a unique and immediate space for displaying the ever-changing programme and needs of contemporary art.

The somewhat labyrinthine circulation works as a revelatory journey of intimate surprises, culminating in a rooftop education suite that is an inspirational delight for the artist in any adult or child.

Section

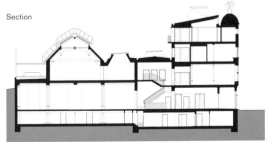

WHITECROSS STREET
EC1

PROJECT ORANGE

CLIENTS: SIMON AND ANNA HOLT
STRUCTURAL ENGINEER: TECHNIKER
CONTRACTOR: BLAKE BUILDERS
CONTRACT VALUE: £700,000
DATE OF COMPLETION: DECEMBER 2008
GROSS INTERNAL AREA: 245 SQ. M
IMAGES: GARETH GARDNER

This eclectic response to the 'bucolic nature of this part of London' (in the words of the architect) comprises a 245-square-metre newbuild family house, the conversion of eighteenth-century buildings into five studio flats, and a renovated office and warehouse. The elevations are collages of balconies, bespoke windows, hand-split oak shakes and standing-seam oxidized copper cladding. Assembled carefully together, these elements add a layered depth and a spatial richness to the whole composition.

Inside, there is a flow of space connecting the generous living spaces; there are also intimate corners and surprising external terraces. The house is re-orientated towards the west, making new visual and physical connections to its local context and animating the adjoining public park.

Section

YEW TREE LODGE
LIDGOULD GROVE, RUISLIP

DUGGAN MORRIS ARCHITECTS

CLIENT: LOOK AHEAD HOUSING AND CARE
STRUCTURAL ENGINEER: MICHAEL HADI ASSOCIATES
SERVICES ENGINEER: AJD DESIGN
CONTRACTOR: DURKAN
CONTRACT VALUE: £1,600,000
DATE OF COMPLETION: NOVEMBER 2008
GROSS INTERNAL AREA: 1190 SQ. M
IMAGES: EDMUND SUMNER – VIEW

This project is an excellent example of how a good architect can transform the ordinary into the extraordinary through a few subtle strategic moves and the careful choice of materials combined with keen attention to detail.

The architect inherited a pedestrian L-shaped pitched-roof scheme that already had planning permission. It moved the project away from the boundary wall to allow light into the main corridor at the rear, created an uplifting double-height entrance with bold yet refined use of colour, and gave every room full-height windows. The result is a building awash with light, providing the tenants with the dignity of generous, high-quality space.

Reference is drawn from the neighbouring Grade II-listed Arts and Crafts building, yet interpreted in an uncompromisingly contemporary way.

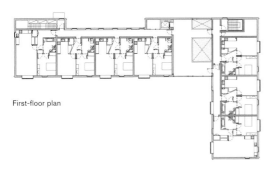

First-floor plan

BRITISH EMBASSY
WARSAW, POLAND

TONY FRETTON ARCHITECTS

CLIENT: FOREIGN AND COMMONWEALTH OFFICE
LANDSCAPE ARCHITECT: SCHOENAICH
STRUCTURAL/SERVICES ENGINEER: BURO HAPPOLD POLSKA
CONTRACTOR: MACE
CONTRACT VALUE: £21,700,000
DATE OF OCCUPATION: SEPTEMBER 2009
GROSS INTERNAL AREA: 4309 SQ. M
IMAGES: PETER COOK – VIEW (TOP; BOTTOM RIGHT); CHRISTIAN RICHTERS –
     VIEW (CENTRE LEFT AND RIGHT; BOTTOM LEFT)

The British Embassy in Warsaw is a careful and intelligent attempt
to rethink the role of this building type. It presents a dignified and
quasi-palatial arrangement of a high central block and two stepped
'wings', in an openly neo-classical reference. The contemporary
difference, however, is that its external skin is an elegant curtain
wall of semi-reflective glass and deep bronzed mullions.

Notably, almost half of the ground floor is given over to spaces
that can be opened up to the public or invited external bodies.
Above are two office floors that can be used in open-plan or cellular
arrangements according to need. A roof terrace is created at
second-floor level, below which two small enclosed atria provide
the users with light and greenery.

CENTRO TECNOLÓGICO PALMAS ALTAS
SEVILLE, SPAIN

ROGERS STIRK HARBOUR + PARTNERS

CLIENT: ABENGOA
STRUCTURAL/SERVICES ENGINEER: ARUP
CONTRACTOR: BOVIS LEND LEASE
CONTRACT VALUE: CONFIDENTIAL
DATE OF OCCUPATION: 2009
GROSS INTERNAL AREA: 48,002 SQ. M
IMAGES: VICTOR SÁJARA

The campus comprises seven stand-alone flexible office buildings, each three to five storeys high, all built around a central plaza, with a nursery, a small shop and staff restaurants. The place-making is complete and well judged. A deep, tree-filled gully divides the discrete buildings on one side from two on the other, which are intended for subletting to other tenants.

Working within a demanding budget, the team has skilfully focused on a limited number of architectural elements, and their refinement and repetition. Floor plans are compact, efficient and flexible. The buildings, however, are far from mundane or repetitive.

The project is Europe's first LEED Platinum-rated development, with energy savings of 40 per cent over a conventional office block; the client sells electricity into the national grid.

Perspective drawing

CUITAT DE LA JUSTÍCIA
BARCELONA AND L'HOSPITALET DE LLOBREGAT, SPAIN

DAVID CHIPPERFIELD ARCHITECTS IN ASSOCIATION WITH B720 ARQUITECTOS

CLIENT: GISA, DEPARTAMENT DE JUSTÍCIA
STRUCTURAL ENGINEERS: JANE WERNICK ASSOCIATES; BOMA
SERVICES ENGINEERS: ARUP; GRUPO JG
CONTRACTOR: URBICSA
CONTRACT VALUE: €240,000,000
DATE OF OCCUPATION: MAY 2009
GROSS INTERNAL AREA: 240,000 SQ. M
IMAGES: CHRISTIAN RICHTERS – VIEW

DCA's approach to what is essentially a huge institutional complex on the suburban fringes of Barcelona, incorporating the City Justice Department, was to break down the 240,000-square-metre programme into a series of nine autonomous towers on and around a central concourse. This site strategy has generated an extraordinarily powerful hybrid: monumental institution with informal urban picturesque.

The simplicity and repetition of the *in-situ* concrete façades are both compelling and mysterious. Each tower varies only in height, orientation and shade of pigmentation, and thus the whole reads as a family of structures. At ground level is a more open, fluid and horizontal space that forms a public route, connecting all the elements of the site.

DCA has produced a highly significant new piece of Barcelona's civic and cultural infrastructure, and one that should be considered a major architectural achievement.

Site plan

HOUSE AT GOLEEN
WEST CORK, IRELAND

NÍALL MCLAUGHLIN ARCHITECTS

CLIENTS: PRIVATE
STRUCTURAL ENGINEER: PRICE & MYERS
SERVICES ENGINEER: ENGINEERING DESIGN CONSULTANTS
CONTRACTOR: CHOM CONSTRUCTION
CONTRACT VALUE: £1,558,790
DATE OF OCCUPATION: JULY 2009
GROSS INTERNAL AREA: 300 SQ. M
IMAGES: NICK GUTTRIDGE – VIEW (TOP RIGHT; CENTRE; BOTTOM);
      NÍALL MCLAUGHLIN (TOP LEFT)
LONGLISTED FOR THE RIBA STIRLING PRIZE

The original slate-roofed, white-rendered house, which faces the sea in a remote part of West Cork, had been extended over the years, resulting in a fragmented plan and disjointed appearance. These additions have been removed, leaving the original cottage to provide an entrance and guest bedrooms. The new house is formed of a series of linear pavilions set parallel to the original, separated by narrow, glazed links and connected by a stepped circulation spine that terminates in a framed view of the sea.

The angular forms have a distinct sculptural quality, and the jumbled composition yields small courtyards that provide shelter from the wind and are camouflaged against the rocky coastline when viewed from the sea. The house is handsome, modest and understated. It is a quiet retreat in a place of great beauty.

Section

189

A.P. MØLLER SKOLEN
SCHLESWIG, GERMANY

ARKITEKTFIRMAET C.F. MØLLER

CLIENT: A.P. MØLLER OG HUSTRU CHASTINE MC-KINNEY MØLLERS FOND TIL
    ALMENE FORMAAL
STRUCTURAL/SERVICES ENGINEER: RAMBØLL DANMARK
CONTRACTOR: OTTO WULFF BAUUNTERNEHMUNG
CONTRACT VALUE: CONFIDENTIAL
DATE OF OCCUPATION: 2008
GROSS INTERNAL AREA: 15,000 SQ. M
IMAGES: POUL IB HENRIKSEN

A.P. Møller Skolen is different both culturally and programmatically from a traditional German school, and serves the Danish community in this northern spur of Germany by day and night.

The principal structure is precast concrete with pale-yellow bricks and big, deep-set windows. A large, copper-clad roof unifies the main arrival/library/dining space with the versatile sports hall at the centre of the plan. The wide stair in the central space provides a venue in which to meet friends and for the school principal to address the pupils. Spaces are flooded with natural light, and the acoustics are excellent.

This flexible and intelligent school serves its community well, and is one any child would enjoy attending.

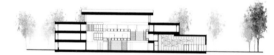

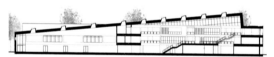

Sections

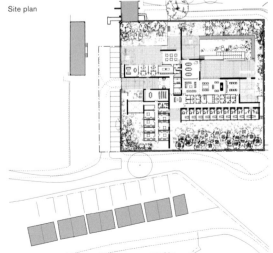

ORCHARD DAY AND RESPITE CARE CENTRE
DUBLIN, IRELAND

NÍALL MCLAUGHLIN ARCHITECTS

CLIENT: THE ALZHEIMER SOCIETY OF IRELAND
STRUCTURAL/SERVICES ENGINEER: BURO HAPPOLD
ACOUSTICS CONSULTANT: PAUL GILLIERON ACOUSTIC DESIGN
CONTRACTOR: LISSADELL CONSTRUCTION
CONTRACT VALUE: £2,700,000
DATE OF OCCUPATION: SEPTEMBER 2008
GROSS INTERNAL AREA: 1392 SQ. M
IMAGES: JOANNA KARATZAS

The pilot project is based on a brief that evolved from the architect's own research into the effects of Alzheimer's disease on people's perception of space, orientation, safety and general comfort. The resulting building is palpably a place of tranquillity and gentle delight. Sited in a historic walled garden, the building consists of a series of pavilions that flow into one another, with new brick walls and timber-and-glass clerestories that bring a majestic quality of light to the spaces even on dreary days.

The architect has created an enclosed world that is at once contained and liberating. The project represents a labour of love for the practice, and it shows in the architecture, which affords everyone time and space – precious healing commodities both.

Site plan

VISUAL CENTRE FOR CONTEMPORARY ART & THE GEORGE BERNARD SHAW THEATRE
CARLOW, IRELAND

TERRY PAWSON ARCHITECTS

CLIENT: CARLOW COUNTY COUNCIL
STRUCTURAL/SERVICES ENGINEER: ARUP DUBLIN
THEATRE CONSULTANT: THEATRE PROJECTS
ACOUSTICS CONSULTANT: ACOUSTIC DIMENSIONS
GALLERY CONSULTANT: BRUCE MCALLISTER
CONTRACTOR: BAM BUILDING (FORMERLY ROHCON)
CONTRACT VALUE: €13,500,000
DATE OF OCCUPATION: SEPTEMBER 2009
GROSS INTERNAL AREA: 3726 SQ. M
IMAGES: HÉLÈNE BINET
LONGLISTED FOR THE RIBA STIRLING PRIZE

VISUAL was conceived as a permanent home for the Éigse, one of Ireland's biggest annual arts festivals. Midway through the design process, a theatre was added to the brief. The architect has responded with some aplomb. The glass-panelled cladding is standard, but well detailed and well handled; the cubic massing of the whole building is aesthetically pleasing and blocky. The project has civic presence, especially at night, when the box glows.

Inside, the plan is simple and legible. Here the materials are primarily concrete and deep-brown wood. The concrete is patterned with engineered wood shuttering — an original touch that is both practical (it hides the imperfections) and visually effective. All in all, this is a building handsomely delivered.

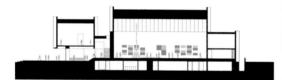

Section

LOOKING BACK,
LOOKING FORWARDS
RT HON. LORD SMITH OF FINSBURY

One of the most important responsibilities of my (relatively) new role as Chairman of the Environment Agency is to ensure that the maintenance and deployment of the Thames Barrier happens in the best possible way. Designed some thirty years ago, the barrier protects London from the impact of tidal surges coming up the Thames Estuary; if it weren't there, the consequences would be unthinkable. I never cease to marvel at the brilliance of the architects and engineers who designed the barrier in the first place. They made it a thing of beauty, not just a functional entity. They ensured there were double and triple fail-safe mechanisms available. And, even though they didn't know anything about climate change, they built it to a standard that will serve us for another seventy years or so, even taking into account the worst current predictions for the rise in sea levels. In other words, they made it better than was strictly necessary at the time – and thank goodness. It's a lesson that we ought to apply rather more often than we do.

The Thames Barrier was opened in 1984. In subsequent years, though, that simple principle of aiming for high quality of design and function seemed to slip away. Reflecting on the architectural record and performance of the past decade, however, I like to think that in many of the major projects that have been undertaken – in both the public and the private sectors – the idea of quality has returned to the fore.

When I became Secretary of State at the Department for Culture, Media and Sport in 1997, the principal guarantor of quality was the Royal Fine Art Commission. It commented on a relatively small number of major projects each year, and did so well. But its impact was limited by its nature and scope, and I felt strongly that something more was needed. So I set up CABE – the Commission for Architecture and the Built Environment – with the remit to raise architectural standards across the board, not just in relation to particular projects. It would be a champion for architectural quality. It would argue that frequently the spaces between the buildings are just as important as the buildings themselves. And, above all, it would look at architecture and the environment it created in a holistic way, understanding and explaining and nurturing the effect on people's lives, the quality of their work, the state of their health and the nature of their well-being. It is a source of pride to me that CABE has been a great success. British architecture is the better for it. Much of the progress we've seen over the past decade is down to the brilliance of the architects involved, but I think CABE has played its part.

The increase in architectural quality of the past decade has, of course, been helped by the flow of funds, from the National Lottery, from the public purse, and from the proceeds of growth in the private sector. The Lottery, in particular, has enabled the creation of a vast range of iconic cultural buildings. There was a period when, as Secretary of State, I seemed to be going from one major cultural opening or foundation-stone-laying to another: the National Portrait Gallery extension one week, the Eden Project the next, the British Museum Great Court,

At-Bristol, the Lowry Centre, the Millennium Bridge on the Tyne, the National Botanic Garden of Wales, Our Dynamic Earth in Edinburgh. Even the dear old Dome (now the O2) was a fabulous building. It got the content wrong – indeed, its major problem was that it was always a building in search of content, and that is the wrong way round to do anything – but as a structure it was, and is, stunning.

Some of the major Lottery projects have struggled, often because of their location. The Botanic Garden in Wales is a case in point: beautiful gardens, fabulous building by Foster + Partners, but not enough visitors. In many cases, however, especially in urban centres, great cultural projects have spurred on a much wider process of regeneration. It's a lesson we learned in the late 1990s from Bilbao, but it is equally true in Salford, from the creation of the Lowry Centre, or in Southwark, from the impact of Tate Modern. Cafes, businesses, shops, galleries, chic flats, offices and hotels begin to spring up, and economic activity and life gradually grow. Sustaining growth, though, is harder than it seems, and frequently depends on getting the little things right, as well as the big iconic ones: the street furniture, the public spaces, the access routes, the maintenance of green areas, and so on. But, by and large, the legacy of the first ten or fifteen years of the Lottery is a wonderful array of great cultural buildings and the life they have brought to the surrounding areas. Full marks to John Major for starting it all off, and to the subsequent government for continuing to deploy it as a way of improving architectural quality throughout the country.

Not everything in the past decade has gone quite so well. I particularly worry about some of the Private Finance Initiative projects that have been put together during the past few years. Where the prime motive has been to decrease cost in order to gain profits for the providers of finance, I fear that the principle of quality may occasionally have been sacrificed. Only time will tell; but if short cuts have been taken at the outset, the iron law of building design tells us that more money will need to be spent in the years to come.

One of the most positive things about architecture and development in the past ten years, however, has been the way in which we've embraced both the creation of exciting new buildings and the renovation of older ones. It's not just such high-profile examples as Tate Modern or Baltic; up and down the country, warehouses have been transformed into flats, mills have been turned into workshops, old factories have been transmogrified, and many other examples of our industrial heritage have been brought into modern use. This wholly positive development has meant that entire areas have been kept intact but brought up to date at the same time. Preserving our heritage buildings in aspic wouldn't have done, but keeping the special qualities of the environment they've created, while pouring new life into them, has been truly impressive.

One of the major themes of the new government is the importance of localism: a sense of place and of community, and the importance of thinking in terms of areas, towns and local districts, rather than regions. Potentially, this approach has huge benefits to offer the world of architecture. When the emphasis is strongly on the locality of a building – the surroundings and immediate context – attention will be more seriously paid to its form and function. Localism must avoid turning into Nimbyism, of course, but it can be a powerful tool in the hands of local communities wanting to shape their built environment.

Function is indeed often as important as form, since it concerns how intelligently a building adapts to its purpose. Perhaps we need to recapture some of the spirit of Colin Stansfield Smith, the great County Architect of Hampshire during the 1980s and 1990s, who designed public buildings with passion and, above all, with intelligence. Many of his schools and libraries have stood the test of time, remaining interesting buildings, but also eminently usable. When designing them, he stumbled across a simple but inspired idea: link the purposes of buildings by providing a number of different public services in one place and you could save money, and perhaps even improve the services at the same time. He sacrificed not quality but the pre-conceived notions of how a school, library or courthouse should look. The result was synergy: a fine collection of well-designed buildings doing several different things. Perhaps, in these straitened financial times, we need to rekindle some of that innovative spirit in order to find ways of enabling buildings to do more than the sum of their parts.

We are faced by two great challenges as we look at what the future will bring for British architecture. The first is precisely the struggle we will all have over the next few years: to maintain the standard and quality of buildings and environments, while costing the public (or private) purse less. We must never forget that high quality delivers better value, and we must resist the temptation to cut corners in order to make a project fit a tight budget, ignoring the consequences later in the life of the building. Times will be especially hard for the public sector, and less building work will happen. But we must make absolutely sure that less building doesn't lead to diminished quality.

The second challenge is the prospect of climate change and its consequences – more floods and more droughts, more constraint on water resources, new patterns of increasingly intensive weather, higher sea levels – and the need for new building design both to adapt to the danger of those consequences and to play its part in alleviating the causes of climate change in the first place. Every building must be designed with low energy use in mind; with thought about the carbon generated by the production of all the materials that go into it; and with a care for its future resilience to floods and weather. But the lesson of those inventive designers of the Thames Barrier must also ring in our ears: even though we don't know precisely what the next fifty or a hundred years will bring, we should design prudently, excellently and with high quality, because that will serve us well in the future.

THE ROYAL GOLD MEDAL

ELIZABETH WALDER, MA, FRSA

The Royal Gold Medal was established by the RIBA in 1848, and is still awarded and celebrated today. It was conceived as a result of a conversation between the then President of the RIBA, Earl de Grey, and Prince Albert.

The idea for a Gold Medal had come about in 1846, twelve years after the foundation of the RIBA. Originally, it was to be awarded to the winner of a competition to encourage young architects to design 'a building suitable and practical to house the Institute and its daily operations' – an idea that received royal approval from Buckingham Palace. Eleven designs were submitted, but – according to the RIBA's centenary history – 'they missed the mark so entirely: they were, most of them, so grandiose and expensive – in short, they so widely disregarded the conditions imposed, that the medal was not awarded. This fiasco sealed the fate of the junior members of the profession in regard to the medal and it was decided to award it in future not to the immature work of the young but in recognition of the actual achievements of the older men [sic].' (In fact, to date, shockingly, no woman has won the medal in her own right.)

Earl de Grey's fresh approach was communicated to Queen Victoria via Prince Albert. It was agreed that the medal should be 'conferred on some distinguished architect for work of high merit, or on some distinguished person whose work has promoted either directly or indirectly the advancement of architecture'. This has remained the basis of the criteria to this day.

The RIBA commissioned William Wyon, Chief Engraver of the Royal Mint, to execute the medal. The Vice-President of the RIBA, Ambrose Poynter, designed the reverse, showing a laurel wreath encircling text and the RIBA's coat of arms. The name of the winner is inscribed around the edge of the medal. Today the Royal Gold Medal is still made by the Royal Mint. As the gift of the monarch, it shares a coveted status with twenty-four other Royal Prize Medals awarded annually by Her Majesty The Queen. As originally conceived, previous winners include architects, engineers, historians, writers and theorists (see pp. 257–59).

Nominations for Royal Gold Medallists are made by members of the RIBA in the first half of the year prior to the year of the award. Names are considered by a distinguished panel chaired by the President of the RIBA and including architects and non-architects from the United Kingdom and overseas. One name is presented to Her Majesty for approval, and the winner is announced in October. The formal presentation is held the following February.

This year's Honours Committee, which chooses the Medallist and the International and Honorary Fellows (see pp. 210–17 and 218–24), comprised the following:

RUTH REED
RIBA PRESIDENT

DAVID ADJAYE, OBE
ARCHITECT, ADJAYE ASSOCIATES

EDWARD CULLINAN, CBE
ARCHITECT, EDWARD CULLINAN ARCHITECTS

MAX FORDHAM
ENVIRONMENTAL ENGINEER, MAX FORDHAM

ANNE LACATON
ARCHITECT, LACATON & VASSALL

LAURA LEE
CLIENT, MAGGIE'S CENTRES

I.M. PEI: THE ROYAL GOLD MEDAL CITATION
DAVID ADJAYE

I.M. Pei's career has been an extraordinary gift to architecture. 'To be a good architect,' he has said, 'there is something about pushing the limit … I would like to think I push myself to the limit.'

Ieoh Ming Pei (commonly known as I.M. Pei) is a Chinese American architect. Born in Guangzhou, China, in 1917, he travelled to the United States in 1935 to study architecture, and has never returned to live in his home country. He graduated from the Massachusetts Institute of Technology (MIT), where Le Corbusier and Alvar Aalto were among the visiting lecturers and professors. He later received a Masters degree from the Harvard Graduate School of Design, where he studied under Walter Gropius and Marcel Breuer, and alongside Philip Johnson, at that time a mature student. In the course of his studies he came under the influence of the International style, which would inspire his work for the next seventy years. One of his projects at Harvard was for a new museum in Shanghai. His design tested the boundaries of Modernism, and was much praised by Gropius, although Pei himself did not care for it. He preferred his MIT thesis, 'Propaganda Units in China', a series of prefabricated units of bamboo with panels painted in different colours to indicate usage: dance, performance, lecture, film. Of the project Pei has said, 'All of these projects were purely speculative. We didn't know what to do. You dreamed. That was my dream then.'

Pei began his architectural practice in the early 1950s, and has produced challenging and thoughtful architecture in every decade since; his work has become a defining part of the period in which it was built. His first commissions were for the noted planner-developer William Zeckendorf. The Miesian Mile High Center in Denver (1952–56), a twenty-three-storey tower, was way ahead of its time, and demonstrated Pei's mature belief that you do not need a lot of money to do good architecture, just a lot of thought. But Zeckendorf was not interested merely in commercial architecture. With Pei as his architect, he would fly from city to city persuading mayors to apply for federal funding for slum clearance and urban renewal – 'healing the wounds of the city', in Pei's telling phrase. The low budgets for such early radical housing and urbanism projects as Kips Bay in New York (1957–62) forced him to experiment with materials. This was architecture of the minimum. Brick was too expensive, so Pei argued for in-situ concrete: the façade was the structure. Kips Bay also gave Pei his first experience of masterplanning, a subject still dear to his heart. He found the original plan produced by Skidmore, Owings & Merrill (SOM) too complex and, with the brilliant arrogance of youth, insisted on two blocks instead of five. Kips Bay still stands today, with Pei's name on a plaque. It is a fine early achievement, a social project that has paid its way in the commercial world; Pei is still immensely proud of it.

Pei's architecture has always asked searching questions, and provided invaluable answers, as to how contemporary architecture can engage with the complex issues of our time. As early as 1954 he was proposing the Hyperboloid, a 457-metre, 108-storey crown-of-thorns skyscraper. The design tapered towards two-thirds height, so that every floorplate was different, before flourishing out to its crown. Its aerodynamic shape made it more resistant to nuclear blast, while underneath was a transport interchange, the likes of which has never been achieved in the United States. And although 70 per cent bigger in volume than the Empire State Building, it would have used the same amount of steel. This was green thinking before its time.

Pei's first major built project in his own name was the National Center for Atmospheric Research in Colorado (1961–67), won in competition against Aalto. Built in the foothills of the Rocky Mountains, it was influenced by a visit that Pei made to the cliff dwellings at Mesa Verde constructed by indigenous Americans in the thirteenth century, which merge into their environment through their use of local materials. Pei's budget did not stretch to stone, but he reconstituted the local rock and then hammered the surface of the pinkish aggregate. Just as influential, although in an entirely negative way, was his visit to SOM's US Air Force Academy at Colorado Springs, where the aluminium and glass played against the setting. Pei chose the other way; by now he was developing his own lexicon.

There followed Pei's first museum, the Everson Museum of Art, in Syracuse, New York (1961–68), which is as sculptural as the pieces it contains. Here, Pei was able to play with form, and the space created by form, for the first time. The museum's success gave him the credibility to undertake what many still consider his masterpiece: the East Building of the National Gallery of Art in Washington, D.C. (1968–78). At last there would be no compromises on site, budget or time. The benefactor, Paul Mellon, considered it the only great work of art he ever commissioned: 'The choice of I.M. Pei as architect was ultimately mine and I shall always be proud that I made that choice.'

Despite the grandeur of its setting on the National Mall, the East Building has an intimacy that makes it better suited to families than the West Building or the Metropolitan Museum of Art in New York – 'My children always preferred the Guggenheim', says Pei. This is in part because of the triangular site and the differing height restrictions, which result in the three house museums, the atrium garden and the constantly shifting perspectives. But it is the introduction of daylight – the massive skylight was an overnight inspiration – that makes the building so memorable. And it was this, together with the triangular form, that Pei took much further with his commission for the Grand Louvre in Paris (1983–93).

Given the cultural sensitivity of the French, the Louvre project was Pei's most difficult. Here he was toying with one of France's greatest icons, but instead of treading carefully, he waded in. He was also up against the public's inability to understand a building until it is complete and they can inhabit it. Yet another problem was that the Louvre lacked the infrastructure required by a modern museum. Pei proposed to excavate the two courtyards to accommodate the necessary facilities. When he asked President Mitterrand for permission, his response was immediate: 'Très bien.' That solved the technical problem, but the public still needed to be enticed in. The glass pyramid was the solution. The Commission Supérieure des Monuments Historiques, to whom Pei had to present, called it 'a fake diamond and very cheap'. Fortunately, his French was not good enough for him to understand, and he persevered. With the support of Mitterrand and Jacques Chirac, the then mayor of Paris, he won over both the nation and the world.

Prior to this came the fulfilment of the personal commission from Jackie Kennedy for the John F. Kennedy Presidential Memorial Library and Museum in Boston (1965–79). 'The client', says Pei, 'not only has to like what you have done, but also you as a person.' It was this relationship that protected the project from the effects of long delays, inflation and numerous site changes. The landfill site chosen for the project was hardly auspicious, but the building suitably memorializes a president who will be forever young. The use of a space frame and the glazing would be seen again in the atrium of Raffles City, Singapore (1973–86), as well as, of course, in the Grand Louvre.

Pei has already been honoured with the American Institute of Architects' Gold Medal (1979), the Pritzker Architecture Prize (1983), the Praemium Imperiale for architecture (1989) and the title of Officier de la Légion d'Honneur (1993). He is also an Honorary Academician of the Royal Academy of Arts, London (1993).

In recent decades Pei has worked on a truly international stage, especially in his homeland of China, creating the vernacular-inspired Fragrant Hill Hotel in Beijing (1979–82), the Bank of China Tower in Hong Kong (1982–89), the Bank of China Head Office in Beijing (1994–2001) and the Suzhou Museum (2000–06). Each of these projects grafts new technologies on to the roots of indigenous building techniques, to create a new, distinctly modern form of Chinese architecture. There have been important European commissions, too: the Deutsches Historisches Museum Zeughaus in Berlin (1996–2003) and the Musée d'Art Moderne in Luxembourg (1995–2006), both of which brought local cultural challenges. Finally, looking again to the East, there have been the

Grand Louvre, Paris, France, 1983–93

Miho Museum in Shiga, Japan (1991–97), and, most recently, the Museum of Islamic Art in Doha, Qatar (2000–08).

When I began my studies in architecture, Pei was already a giant in the canon of greats. His work seemed effortlessly capable of creating extraordinary clarity out of complex and conflicting demands. His is an agile ability: he has worked with heads of state, kings and queens, with 'hard-nosed' developers and not-for-profit institutions, in each case producing revealing, extraordinary works of precision with quality and detail.

I remember as a young student first visiting the Louvre in Paris and marvelling at how Pei's work had succeeded in unifying and modernizing what was a much-loved but disparate institution, especially his magnificent, gravity-defying glass pyramid. He became a role model for me as a young architect.

In recent years I have been able to visit his early housing and urbanism works, and have been struck by his ability to create humane and high-quality architecture with minimal means, at extremely low costs – a valuable lesson for our times.

Grand Louvre, Paris, France, 1983–93

Museum of Islamic Art, Doha, Qatar, 2000–08

I.M. PEI IN CONVERSATION WITH DAVID ADJAYE

DAVID ADJAYE TALKED TO I.M. PEI AT HIS HOME IN NEW YORK FOLLOWING THE ANNOUNCEMENT OF THE NINETY-TWO-YEAR-OLD CHINESE AMERICAN'S SUCCESSFUL NOMINATION FOR THE 2010 ROYAL GOLD MEDAL.

DA: I'd like to talk about the influence of Chinese culture on your architecture.

PEI: I can't think of anything that influenced me to the extent that I became an architect. It's just my family had always been interested in the arts. My mother was a painter and a poet. My father was a banker; they were very different in that sense. Also, my family came from Suzhou, which is famous for its gardens. So I came from that kind of background. That means that I should have a certain appreciation for the arts – but that may not be the case. But there is something that I did inherit, and I am very proud of it.

DA: You went on to study in the United States, which was the most extraordinary image of Modernism at that time.

PEI: I am always fascinated by the West. And it wasn't so much the education that I was looking to; I was looking forward to seeing something entirely new. And all my life I'd lived in China and never been outside a very small confined area. So it's only natural that I would fancy myself going somewhere far away. And I had my wish … I would say that the Modern Movement was ingrained in me because of the personalities that I associated with. I consider myself a second generation after Gropius, Breuer and Aalto.

DA: Were you aware of the power of Modernism, and that somehow it would define the twentieth century?

PEI: I don't think so. I knew that I was among people who were very influential in the Modern Movement; I was aware of that. But I didn't really place myself in that situation. I thought I was very fortunate to be able to learn from these masters, but they turned out to be more than masters to me; they turned out to be friends. That's the important thing in my life.

DA: After the Second World War you very quickly started working with developers, and you started building extraordinary urban projects. I'm thinking especially of New York

and several other places. Can you tell us about that amazing time?

PEI: When you are thinking about urban renewal, you are not thinking about buildings; you are talking about slum clearance, how to revitalize a very decayed part of the city, how to heal the wounds. And you have to be young and altruistic, and I was then.

DA: I went to see Kips Bay recently, and I was shocked at how immaculate it was. The detailing is still perfect.

PEI: Really?

DA: And the apartments, how beautifully kept they are, and how much of an urban oasis the gardens are, and how loved by the residents.

PEI: This is music to my ears. Kips Bay is very important to me because I had nothing to show at that time in New York, and when I had that opportunity working for Zeckendorf, and he had a chance to buy that property, he asked me, what do you think we can do with it? And at that time Kips Bay was a very derelict area, a very poor neighbourhood. But Kips Bay is big enough to create an environment of its own. It has enough acreage so that you can create not only a space but also a community. So from the very beginning we looked upon Kips Bay not as a single piece of architecture but as an organic whole to create a community.

DA: Can you tell us about the Society Hill project in Philadelphia?

PEI: Society Hill at that time was a dilapidated area, so to turn it over in a very short time, to something that is – you can almost see the result in a short time – that was a very good example of what urban redevelopment can do. I remember. And it really takes a combination of civic and professional leadership; luckily, Society Hill had it. We added many new town houses to the old, so it's not only building new towers but it's also

Luce Memorial Chapel, Taichung, Taiwan, 1954–63

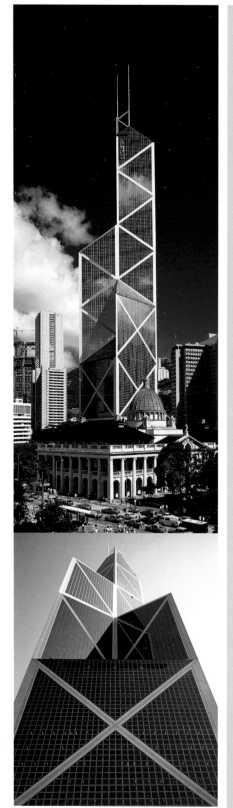

Bank of China Tower, Hong Kong, 1982–89

adding new ones to the old town houses to complete the cityscape. I would consider it one of the more successful urban-redevelopment projects. Urban redevelopment usually takes time, and this one was accomplished in a matter of five or six years. So in that sense I think it's considered a success.

DA: I want to talk now about your museums, which to me, in many ways, are some of your most beautiful works. Can I ask you about, I think, one of your greatest projects, the East Building project? For me, you've created a new typology of how to use museums of the past, and shown how they could display work in the future.

PEI: I think, before that, there's also the question of formulating a future direction for architecture, because, until then, John Russell Pope, who did the original wing of the National Gallery, was really a standard for us all to look at – neo-classic. The East Building, I would say, is a break from that tradition, and my challenge was how do you make that break and not lose the connection? I never wanted to be a revolutionary – I really didn't want to be – and I like to evolve along those lines, and therefore the East Building and the original West Building were something that was very much in my mind; I wanted somehow to join the two. There's not meant to be some kind of sharp cut from one to the other. And to join the Modern Movement with the movement of the past, with the neo-classic, is something that's a challenge that I assume to try to do, to make that kind of a connection. So I was not a revolutionary.

DA: Do you think that doing that project influenced the way you came to think about the Louvre, which was the next great challenge in terms of museums?

PEI: I think the East Building is a new building; the Louvre, on the other hand, was not. So therefore I think that, in the East Building, I was free to create and to make the connection really underground. But the Louvre is something where I had to take into consideration the long, long history before. So the question, the challenge, was very different.

DA: It was, and if one was a new building, an object, the other one was making a connection, making a new kind of building, which was not form but spaces –

PEI: Not only spaces in the internal services, but also external space; it was the making of the public space that was the challenge of the Louvre. The Louvre before that was just a scattering of objects on the Parisian scene. And I tried to join them together to make them whole, so in some ways the real challenge was the public space where the pyramid is. And at least I did something there that tells you what the Louvre is today.

DA: I wanted to contrast the Louvre with a project that wasn't built: the Hyperboloid.

PEI: Ah, I never built that building.

DA: I know …

PEI: That's Grand Central Station.

DA: Exactly.

PEI: The Hyperboloid … I remember very well how Zeckendorf and I were working on that one together. So he arranged for Robert Moses to listen to my spiel about the project on a train from somewhere uptown from New York, and ride all the way down to Grand Central. I had about an hour and a half to sell the idea to Mr Moses. I didn't succeed … That's one building I wish I had built, you are right; I would have liked to build that building.

DA: I'd like to ask you about the JFK project. I know it was a long-drawn-out project, but it's an important one, and I'd love to hear your thoughts on it.

PEI: Very sad that project, sad. It started with such a promise, just like his life, but then as time went on it fizzled, and I consider the project as one of my less successful, unfulfilled projects. Yes, it was built, but how long did it take? Fourteen years, and during those fourteen years the name Kennedy has gone up and come down; can you imagine? Only fourteen years. In the beginning nickels and dimes from children were filling the coffers, but within a matter of months, and toward the end, very few people were even interested in it. A memorial is something that has to be of the moment, and as time passes people's memories also fade, and I saw that happen in that project with great sadness. It started with great excitement and great promise, and it ended that way. I remember Jackie Kennedy – she was so important in this one. And there were very exciting moments at the beginning of that project, very exciting. We went all over the Eastern Seaboard to look for a site, and in the beginning everybody wanted us. Towards the end we were turned down; Harvard turned us down. Finally, we ended up in South Boston. It shows you something about memory: people's memories are very short.

DA: I'd also like to pick up on the New York University residential towers, in particular the relationship between art and architecture that is so striking there. It has the famous Picasso sculpture.

PEI: I remember I went to see him about it. And I got his permission, that's number one. And then the question was, how big and how to position them? I remember I made a maquette to show him, and so I did get an approval before I proceeded – I went to the South of France.

DA: And did he comment on the buildings? Was he interested in the architecture?

PEI: Not the architecture, but the formal positioning of the towers; no details. I then showed him the environment in which the piece would be, and it was approved. He said, it's fine, go ahead and do it. At that time he was quite – South of France, you know – he was at the end of his life. I know how he felt; he was very – he couldn't possibly be involved any more.

DA: But it was amazing that you met him.

PEI: Yes, I know. That was an experience.

DA: So, can I ask: I.M. Pei, what next, at this time in your life, what next?

PEI: Rest (*laughs*), rest. No, I – I have a chapel in Japan. I started my professional life with a chapel in China, and I think my last project is also a chapel, but this time in Japan. I started with a chapel, I end with a chapel.

Pavilion, Oare House, Wiltshire, England, 1999–2003

National Center for Atmospheric Research, Colorado, Denver, 1961–67

DA: I hope that's not the story, but I understand professionally – I understand the process.

PEI: Oh, professionally, yes it is, because if I am not doing anything now, nothing will be built in the next five years. No, you have to start now if you want to see something five years hence. I stopped some time ago, so I can say that; that will be my last work.

DA: And that's a beautiful chapel –

PEI: Well, I've done enough, I guess (*laughs*).

DA: And finally, Mr Pei, what does winning the Royal Gold Medal mean to you?

PEI: Ah, very satisfying, really. I no longer expect to receive any medals – after all, I long since stopped my work – and especially coming from England, because I am not particularly well known in Great Britain. I am well known in the Far East and Japan, in France, but not in England. So to be recognized in England is something I rather prize, I think – well, you are from England. I was not trained there; I was trained in the United States. And I wasn't very active lecturing, as some architects do. So therefore I was surprised that the RIBA even chose me, but I am very proud of that, very proud.

Everson Museum of Art, Syracuse, New York, 1961–68

East Building, National Gallery of Art, Washington, D.C., 1968–78

Suzhou Museum, Jiangsu, China, 2000–06

Morton H. Meyerson Symphony Center, Dallas, Texas, 1981–89

THE RIBA
INTERNATIONAL FELLOWSHIPS

Throughout its 176-year history, the RIBA has honoured men and women who have made a major contribution to the world of design and, in particular, architecture. Any architect outside the United Kingdom who is not a UK citizen, has a demonstrable interest in the objectives of the RIBA, and exhibits distinction and breadth of contribution to architecture may be elected an International Fellow of the RIBA. Prior to 2006, such people were elected Honorary Fellows; in 2006, with the creation of the new honour, all architect Honorary Fellows, including non-UK surviving Royal Gold Medallists, were made RIBA International Fellows.

Of the ten architects made International Fellows in 2010, six work in partnership. They come from seven different countries in four different continents, and their work not only represents the spirit of their countries, but also transcends it to become truly international in its reference and influence.

This year's RIBA International Fellows were chosen by the Honours Committee, which also selects the Royal Gold Medallist and the RIBA Honorary Fellows (see pp. 198–209 and 218–24). For the list of committee members, see p. 198.

ALEJANDRO ARAVENA
(CHILE)

Alejandro Aravena was born in 1967, and studied at the Universidad Católica de Chile in Santiago, where he now teaches. He set up in practice in 1994, and since 2006 has been executive director of Elemental SA. Instead of building up an office, he collaborates with other architects on a project-by-project basis. He describes his practice as a 'do tank' (as opposed to a think tank) that 'contributes to improve the quality of life in Chilean cities, providing state-of-the-art architecture and engineering, understanding the city as an unlimited resource to build social equity'.

Aravena's work in Chile includes House for a Sculptor (1997), House on Pirehueico Lake (2004) and the Quinta Monroy (social housing) in Iquique (2004), as well as social housing and urban projects for Elemental, working with civil engineer Andrés Iacobelli on prefabricated housing systems; the Huelquen Montessori School (2001); and the Mathematics Faculty (1999), the Medical Faculty (2004), the School of Architecture (2004) and the Siamese Towers (2005) for the Universidad Católica. His work outside of Chile includes the new residence and dining hall for St Edward's University in Austin, Texas (2008), and new children's workshops and training facilities for the Vitra furniture company in Weil am Rhein in Germany (2008). Aravena was recently one of a hundred architects from twenty-seven countries invited by Herzog & de Meuron to take part in the Ordos 100, a project in which each architect was given one hundred days to create a 1000-square-metre house in Ordos, Inner Mongolia, China. For his work at St Edward's University he took inspiration from the work done by Alvaro Aalto and Louis Kahn on other college campuses.

In 2009 Aravena won the Marcus Prize for emerging talents. He has previously won a prize at the Venice Biennale, and has been a finalist in the Mies van der Rohe Award (2000) and in the Global Award for Sustainable Architecture (2008).

Aravena is the author of three books on architecture, and has had his work published in the United States, the United Kingdom, Italy, Germany, Portugal, The Netherlands, France, Russia and China. His work has been exhibited in São Paulo, Milan and Venice, and at Harvard University in Massachusetts.

Siamese Towers, Universidad Católica de Chile, Santiago, 2005

ELIZABETH DILLER AND RICARDO SCOFIDIO (USA)

Diller Scofidio + Renfro is a New York City-based architectural firm founded by Elizabeth Diller and Ricardo Scofidio. Diller was born in Lodz, Poland, and studied at New York City's Cooper Union School of Architecture. She is now a professor at Princeton. Scofidio was born in New York City and also studied at Cooper Union, where he is a professor emeritus. As a practice, they take an interdisciplinary approach to architecture. Their influence stems as much, if not more, from their contributions to the theory and criticism of architecture (in written work, but more often in the form of installation art, video art or electronic art) as from their built works. Charles Renfro joined the practice in 1997 and was made a partner in 2004.

Diller and Scofidio began working in the 1980s, on set designs and installations. Their first built work was the Slow House, a modest private residence on Long Island, completed in 1991. For the Swiss Expo 2002, they built the Blur Building, a lake pavilion entirely enveloped in mist; more than 30,000 jets sprayed drops of lake water so small that most remained suspended in the air. This 'fleeting sculpture'

was visible in all weathers. In 2003 Diller and Scofidio were the subject of a major retrospective at the Whitney Museum of American Art, *Scanning: The Aberrant Architectures of Diller + Scofidio*. The firm also designed the new building for the Institute of Contemporary Art in Boston (2006), and worked on the redevelopment of Lincoln Center for the Performing Arts in New York City. In the summer of 2009 it opened the High Line, a park in New York City built on a stretch of an abandoned elevated-train viaduct 6 metres above the street.

Diller and Scofidio demonstrate how new ways of thinking can cut across the divide and become mainstream and relevant. As practitioners, from their early speculations within academia to their recently realized projects, they have remained committed to the highest level of thinking and design, and they are an inspiration at a time when the quality of ideas is always under pressure. As cultural theorists, they have a duty to remind us that architecture is everywhere.

Institute of Contemporary Art, Boston, 2006

YVONNE FARRELL AND SHELLEY MCNAMARA (IRELAND)

Yvonne Farrell and Shelley McNamara are directors of Grafton Architects, which since its inception in 1978 has been one of Ireland's leading practices and is one of the most significant female-led practices in Europe.

Grafton Architects is recognized nationally and internationally for the production of buildings and urban interventions of a consistently high standard, and has won more than twenty awards and several competitions. The practice's work has been exhibited in Paris, Zurich, Madrid, Barcelona (under the auspices of the European Union Prize for Contemporary Architecture – Mies van der Rohe Award), London and at the 2002 Venice Architecture Biennale, and has featured in many international publications.

Grafton Architects has developed a rigorous and sensitive approach to building in the city, believing strongly that careful research is crucial in order that latent urban potential be nurtured in a manner that sustains and builds upon places' essential character. This expertise has been developed through significant projects in a wide range of complex urban and social situations. Grafton Architects, as a founding member of Group 91 Architects, played a central role in the regeneration of Dublin's Temple Bar through participation in the formulation of the framework plan and the design and construction of the Temple Bar Square building and public space. In recent years, the practice has undertaken several projects and competitions at a scale demanding the development of frameworks for urban intervention. These projects incude social housing in North King Street, in South Earl Street and in Ballymun; the Solstice Arts Centre in Navan; new government offices on St Stephen's Green; and several bridge and transport infrastructure projects.

Grafton Architects' Università Commerciale Luigi Bocconi building in Milan, Italy, was named the first World Building of the Year at the World Architecture Festival 2008 in Barcelona. In 2009 it was also the first building by an Irish practice to become a finalist in the European Union Prize for Contemporary Architecture – Mies van der Rohe Award. The university building is really a piece of city, fronting on to a busy street and providing a window on the students' activities in the market place within.

Università Commerciale Luigi Bocconi, Milan, Italy, 2008

FRANCIS KÉRÉ
(BURKINA FASO/GERMANY)

Francis Kéré is a young architect from Burkina Faso in West Africa who studied in Germany. During his studies, with the assistance of his friends, he founded the Schulbausteine für Gando association, the main aims of which are to create buildings that meet climatic demands, and to support the Burkinan people in their development.

Since 1999 Kéré has taken part in numerous national and international conferences and has given lectures at several European universities. The projects he has run since 2001 as an independent designer are situated worldwide, from Burkina Faso to India.

A primary school that Kéré designed for his home village of Gando won the prestigious Aga Khan Award for Architecture in 2004, and in 2009 he was a finalist in the Global Award for Sustainable Architecture, the purpose of which is 'to honour annually five living architects who move towards sustainability'.

Besides his occupation as a self-employed planner, Kéré has worked as a lecturer in the Habitat Unit at the Technische Universität Berlin since 2004. His main subjects are housing and urban development, strategies of climatically advantageous building, the sustainable use of materials, integration of the local labour force and local construction techniques. He has also considered these topics in numerous articles and chapters in international specialist journals and books.

Kéré does not limit himself to architecture, however. Through his association, he tries to provide the people of his homeland with innovative development projects that will offer them better prospects. This means providing facilities for adult education, health care, and economic support for women, who bear the greatest share of family and social burdens in his country. Consequently, his motto is 'help to self-help'. Kéré is not an architect who imposes his ideas and his methods on others; instead, he works with people to build houses and schools that will, as he modestly puts it, 'survive several rainy seasons'.

Kéré is a role model for all architects who aspire to use the term 'sustainable' to describe their work.

Primary School, Gando, Burkina Faso, 1999

VALERIO OLGIATI
(SWITZERLAND)

Valerio Olgiati was born in 1958 and studied architecture at the Eidgenössische Technische Hochschüle (ETH) Zürich. Having lived and worked first in Zurich and later for some years in Los Angeles, he opened his own practice in Zurich in 1996, and in Flims in 2008.

Olgiati's projects in Switzerland include the Yellow House in Flims (1995–99), formerly the house of his architect father, Rudolf. Olgiati gutted the building and stripped it back to stone, then painted it white according to his father's wishes, although the building retained its original name. His House for a Musician in Scharans (2005–07) occupies just one-third of the footprint of the old barn it replaced; this 'missing volume' is defined by red concrete walls that are embossed with abstract patterns. The striking black exterior and interiors of Olgiati's architectural office at Flims (2008) make for a better appreciation of the exterior world from within, creating more extrovert, public spaces. His museum for the Swiss National Park in Zernez (2009), with its unique spatial mirroring, is made of white concrete with bronze detailing. Olgiati's National Palace Museum in Taiwan (2004) is built around two courtyards, at the heart of each of which is a pool. Still to come is

Perm XXI, a competition-winning entry for a museum in Perm, Russia, that appears to mark a new direction.

In 2009 Olgiati gave one of the lectures in the Le Corbusier talks series at the RIBA, discussing four projects, three built and one unbuilt. An accompanying exhibition, also at the RIBA, based on seven schemes, explored Olgiati's rigorous conceptual design framework through a series of spectacular plaster models at a scale of 1:33, accompanied by photographs and renderings.

Olgiati was awarded the German Architecture Prize Appreciation Honour in 1993; he has been awarded the prize for the Best Building in Switzerland three times, and in 2001 he received the Swiss Concrete Award. He has taught as a guest professor at ETH Zürich, London's Architectural Association School of Architecture and Cornell University, New York State. Since 2002 he has been a professor at the Accademia di Architettura di Mendrisio at the Università della Svizzera Italiana.

Lake Cauma Project, Flims, Switzerland, 2002

PAUL ROBBRECHT AND HILDE DAEM (BELGIUM)

Paul Robbrecht works with Hilde Daem in the Robbrecht en Daem architecture practice in Ghent. The two have a strong interest in the development of visual arts and their possible influence on architecture. In the 1970s, when Robbrecht and Daem started their practice, they succeeded in re-evaluating architecture as an autonomous discipline. Their inspiration came from contemporary art as well as from the classical architecture tradition. Their first notable work, a bank building in Kerksken, Belgium, shows their particular interest in classical architectural language. In the Mys House, Oudenaarde, the rooms were modelled in co-operation with artists Thierry de Cordier, Juán Muños and Cristina Iglesias. They then worked with other artists to organize exhibitions. In several projects Robbrecht and Daem focused on the possible relation between art and architecture, including at the Xavier Hufkens gallery in Brussels (1989, with Marie-José Van Hee) and the Aue Paviljoens at Documenta IX (Kassel, 1990–92).

Among Robbrecht and Daem's most important works are the extension and renovation of the Museum Boymans Van Beuningen, Rotterdam (1996–2003), and the Bruges Concertgebouw (1999–2002). The work on Museum Boymans Van Beuningen added several galleries and offices to the east side and created a new entrance. The aim of the project was to make the building smaller – to remove the agglomeration of extensions and to reorder the internal infrastructure, making new relationships between spaces, so as to make it easier for visitors to find their way around. With the concert hall in Bruges the architects have, in architecture critic Jeremy Melvin's words, 'created a wholly sensory experience for their concert-going audience, which embraces the ephemeral quality of musical performance with the physicality of architecture'.

Robbrecht and Daem's rejuvenation of the Whitechapel Gallery in London (see p. 183) – reopened to critical acclaim in 2009 and longlisted for the 2010 RIBA Stirling Prize – doubled the gallery's space and started a debate on the way in which architectural modesty can bring a critical strength to our built environment.

Robbrecht and Daem's architecture demonstrates persistence and duration, and sets a course in opposition to the ephemeral and sensational.

Robbrecht has taught at the Gentse Academie and at Sint-Lucas, both in Ghent, and at the Architectural Association School of Architecture in London.

Robbrecht is an architect with a strong signature. His designs are often the result of an intensive collaboration between the architect, artists and the client. Their essentially humane architecture is a successful cross between science and art.

Whitechapel Gallery, London, 2009

BENEDETTA TAGLIABUE
(ITALY/SPAIN)

Benedetta Tagliabue was born in Milan, and graduated from the Università IUAV di Venezia in 1989. In 1991 she joined Enric Miralles's studio in Barcelona, eventually becoming a partner. Her work with Miralles, whom she married, includes a number of high-profile buildings and projects in Barcelona.

In 1998 the partnership won the competition to design the new Scottish Parliament building in Edinburgh and, despite Miralles's premature death in 2000, Tagliabue took leadership of the team as joint project director. The building was completed in 2004 and has won several awards. Tagliabue's Santa Caterina Market (2005), in the heart of medieval Barcelona, houses a hundred market stalls on three levels, under a beautiful wave-like roof supported by writhing steel columns and dressed with 325,000 multicoloured ceramic tiles. From the surrounding balconies the roof resembles a carpet that is having the dust shaken out of its colourful weave. Her Gas Natural office (2008), a finalist in the first World Architecture Festival awards (2008), responds to the different scales of the nearby apartment buildings by forming a 'doorway' to the Barceloneta neighbourhood and produces a singular public space. The treatment of the façades protects the building from the sun and noise, and makes it appear to dematerialize.

Today, under Tagliabue's direction, the Miralles Tagliabue EMBT studio works on architectural projects, open spaces, urbanism, rehabilitation and exhibitions, trying to conserve the spirit of the Spanish and Italian artisan architectural studio tradition that espouses collaboration rather than specialization. The jobs won during Miralles's lifetime are now complete, and the team Tagliabue leads is winning new and different commissions. The practice's architectural philosophy pays special attention to context: for instance, the Spanish Pavilion for Expo 2010 Shanghai (see p. 69) developed the local handicraft of wicker-weaving into a practical construction technique.

Tagliabue has written for several architectural magazines, and teaches at the School of Architecture of Barcelona (ETSAB). She has exhibited in Brazil, Venezuela, the United States, France, Italy and, of course, Spain. She has received an honorary doctor of arts degree from Napier University in Edinburgh, and in 2005 won the RIBA Stirling Prize and the Spanish National Architecture Prize, both for the Scottish Parliament building. Tagliabue was a brilliant speaker at the RIBA's international conference in Barcelona in 2008 and an outspoken Stirling Prize judge in 2009.

Santa Caterina Market, Barcelona, 2005

THE RIBA HONORARY FELLOWSHIPS

In 2010 the RIBA awarded twelve new Honorary Fellowships to men and women from a wide range of backgrounds, including journalists, clients, engineers, educators and landscape architects.

RIBA Honorary Fellowships reward the particular contributions people have made to architecture in its broadest sense: its promotion, administration and outreach; its role in building more sustainable communities; and finally its role in the education of future generations. The lifetime honour, conferred annually, allows recipients to use the initials Hon FRIBA after their name.

All of these people, be they practitioners or commentators, have done much for architecture. In their very different ways, they have all helped to improve the quality of design and influence the delivery of the built environment in a sustainable and creative way.

This year's RIBA Honorary Fellows were chosen by the Honours Committee, which also selects the Royal Gold Medallist and the RIBA International Fellows (see pp. 198–209 and 210–17). For the list of committee members, see p. 198.

DAVID BIRKBECK
CHIEF EXECUTIVE OF DESIGN FOR HOMES

David Birkbeck probably knows more about housing than most house builders, developers, architects, planners or politicians – representatives of which are partners in the Housing Design Awards, which Birkbeck has ably administered for the past five years. Architectural standards have improved since Birkbeck took over the awards' administration from the RIBA, not least because he is a great proponent of the idea that architects are essential to the design of good housing. He has also professionalized the printed materials and the event associated with the awards. But most significantly it is the depth and breadth of his knowledge, and the quality of the research undertaken by his organization (which grew out of the RIBA's own Housing Group), that have increased the standing of the Housing Design Awards, including among politicians and their advisers.

Birkbeck was a journalist before helping to set up Design for Homes in 2000 as a not-for-profit organization that would research and promote the value of good design in housing. He set out to transform endless design advice into easily applicable information, in keeping with the organization's aim to spread design awareness. Birkbeck feels that homes should be better designed and better built, and in greater volumes, and Design for Homes's research looks at how to do this. The need to strike a balance between what consumers appear to want and what the professionals want to give them underpins much of the organization's output.

In addition to being both the rapporteur and a judge for the Housing Design Awards, Birkbeck was a judge in John Prescott's Design for Manufacture competition to build family homes for £60,000, as well as in the Carbon Challenge to build sustainable homes. Birkbeck runs the Building for Life office for the Commission for Architecture and the Built Environment (CABE) and the Home Builders Federation, and is a board member of the Housing Forum.

PETER BISHOP
PLANNER AND DIRECTOR OF DESIGN FOR LONDON

Peter Bishop is Director of Design for London. He trained in town planning at the University of Manchester, and has spent his entire career working in London. Over the past twenty years he has been a planning director in four different central London boroughs. Major projects he has worked on include Canary Wharf, the development of the BBC's campus at White City and the King's Cross development, one of the largest and most complex sites in London. He was appointed as the first Director of Design for London in 2006 and, in 2008, as Group Director of the London Development Agency, responsible for design, land development, and the agency's environmental, housing and public space programmes.

Bishop navigates the complex urban landscape of London with skill and calm tenacity. Seemingly magically, he manages to turn what appear to be intractable problems into opportunities, where design is placed to the fore and delivery is paramount. His support for the dissemination of new ideas has been much appreciated by the architectural community. On taking on his role at Design for London, Bishop described it as the best job in the world. He believes that there has been a tendency for people to consider the importance of design in an architectural project only once it is too late; in fact, he says, if design is not high on the agenda at the start of a project, it tends not to feature at all. Ever the diplomat, he is aware that his organization has to add value to other people's work without treading on any toes, duplicating effort or making anyone's life more difficult. This sensitivity has enabled him to adapt, survive and succeed in a very changed political climate.

Bishop lectures and teaches extensively, and is a visiting professor at Nottingham Trent University's Faculty of Architecture and the Built Environment.

PATRICK BLANC
LANDSCAPE DESIGNER AND BOTANIST

Ten years ago Frenchman Patrick Blanc began designing eco-conscious architecture for public spaces, department stores and private domestic spaces. He came up with a method of covering both interior and exterior walls with a wide variety of exotic plant species, which previously it had not been possible to grow in such climates or on vertical surfaces. Before this was made possible, the only greening of façades came from climbers, such as mortar-destroying ivy, planted in the soil at the base of walls. Blanc's vertical garden system – or *mur végétal* – allows plants and buildings to work together in harmony. His method can be applied in any climatic environment.

Apart from its aesthetic function, the vertical garden has other natural benefits, such as improving air quality, reducing energy consumption through thermal insulation, providing a natural shield between a space's inhabitants and the elements outside, and introducing biodiversity to the heart of a city.

Blanc has worked with many architects, including Jean Nouvel, Francis Soler and Herzog & de Meuron, on buildings around the world, but he is probably best known for his vertical garden on the façade of Nouvel's Musée du Quai Branly in Paris. Nouvel has said disarmingly of the project: 'When you put in little flowers, people are happy.' The *New York Times* has written of it: 'The exterior of the administration building is swallowed up by a vertical carpet of exotic plants punctured by big windows. On some stories, the plants invade the building, crawling down the interior walls.'

Blanc has also grown his own wallpaper at home and even created a 'green' dress, 'Robe Végétale', that appeared in a Jean Paul Gaultier fashion show in 2002.

SEBASTIAN COE
CHAIR OF THE LONDON ORGANISING COMMITTEE
OF THE OLYMPIC GAMES 2012

Lord Coe is awarded an RIBA Honorary Fellowship for his work in leading the successful bid to host the Olympic Games of 2012 in London. It has resulted in one of the greatest regeneration projects ever seen in the United Kingdom, which will bring a permanent legacy to a neglected area of the city.

Coe is committed to delivering good architecture – a field in which he has been interested since achieving success in technical drawing at the age of fifteen.

Coe is a former top-level athlete and Conservative Party politician. In his athletics career he won the gold medal for the 1500 metres race at the Olympic Games of 1980 and 1984, and set eight outdoor and three indoor world records. He was awarded an MBE in 1982 and an OBE in 1990. Following his retirement from athletics, Coe served as an MP from 1992 to 1997, and became a life peer in 2000. He was the head of the London bid to

host the 2012 Olympic Games and, after this was successful, became Chairman of the London Organising Committee of the Olympic Games. He was made a CBE in 2006 for services to sport.

Owing in part to Coe's influence, sustainability was at the heart of the bid, with a commitment to maximize sustainability through all the phases of the Games: building the venues and infrastructure, staging the Games themselves and then, long into the future, focusing on five key areas (combating climate change; reducing waste; enhancing biodiversity; promoting inclusion; and improving healthy living). Coe sees the London Games as a fantastic platform from which to highlight such vital global issues as climate change.

Coe's cross-party, non-partisan approach to the job in hand has done much to ensure the successful delivery of this great project.

ALAIN DE BOTTON
WRITER

Alain de Botton was born in Zurich, Switzerland, in 1969, and now lives in London. He started writing at a young age, and his first book, *Essays in Love* (1993), was published when he was twenty-three.

De Botton is a writer of books that have been described as a 'philosophy of everyday life'. He has written on love, travel, architecture and literature. His titles have been bestsellers in thirty countries. De Botton also founded and helps to run a school in London called the School of Life, offering programmes touching on issues concerning how to live wisely and well.

De Botton's book *The Pleasures and Sorrows of Work* (2009) celebrates 'an activity as central to a good life as love – but which we often find remarkably hard to reflect on properly'. In the summer of 2009 De Botton spent a week at Heathrow Airport's Terminal 5, designed by Richard Rogers's practice, in order to produce his latest book, *A Week at the Airport: A Heathrow Diary* (2009). Outside of writing, De

Botton has been involved in making a number of television documentaries, and now helps to run a TV production company, Seneca Productions.

De Botton delivered the RIBA Annual Lecture in 2006, basing his address on the themes of his book *The Architecture of Happiness* (2006). The book starts from the idea that where we are influences strongly who we can be, and argues that it is architecture's task to stand as an eloquent reminder of our full potential. Citing examples widely spread both geographically and historically, De Botton posits that good buildings increase our chances of happiness, and that whereas it was once assumed that good architecture equalled classical architecture, in these days of stylistic diversity Philip Johnson's Glass House or S333's Dutch social housing is just as likely to cheer us up as Palladio's Villa Rotunda or the Royal Crescent in Bath.

De Botton was a witty and incisive RIBA Stirling Prize juror in 2007.

TOM DYCKHOFF
JOURNALIST AND BROADCASTER

Tom Dyckhoff is a writer, broadcaster and critic on architecture, cities and design. He is architecture critic at *The Times* and a regular presenter on BBC2's *Culture Show*. In 2009, also for BBC2, he charted the development of the conservation movement since the Second World War in the series *Saving Britain's Past*, in which he examined our current attitudes to heritage with programmes on the conservation of Bath, Covent Garden in London, the country house, our industrial past and Sheffield's 1960s 'streets in the sky' at Park Hill housing estate.

Dyckhoff's other television work includes *I Love Carbuncles* (Channel 4, 2005), *Grand Designs: Trade Secrets* (Channel 4/More 4, 2007–08) and *The Culture Show Goes to China* (BBC2, 2008). He has also contributed to Channel 4's coverage of the RIBA Stirling Prize, and co-presented the BBC's first programme about the prize in 2010. He acted as an ebullient master of ceremonies for the Stirling Prize dinners in 2009 and 2010.

Dyckhoff studied geography before switching to architecture but never completed his training as an architect, preferring to work as a curator and writer in the field. He was a curator in the RIBA's Architecture Gallery in the late 1990s before switching to full-time journalism.

Dyckhoff is a born communicator, in print as well as in person and on television. Just as he is in demand from both Channel 4 and the BBC, so great is his popularity with print editors that he is one of those rare species: a journalist who works simultaneously for two national newspapers, as architecture critic for *The Times* and as a columnist for *The Guardian*.

Dyckhoff's popular appeal rests on his natural wit, boyish charm and ability to explain complex issues in simple language. Architecture needs more Dyckhoffs.

ROLF FEHLBAUM
CLIENT AND CHAIRMAN OF VITRA

Rolf Fehlbaum is Chairman of Vitra, a Swiss company best known for manufacturing chairs. For all his modesty, he is also a visionary. Three years after taking over as chairman in 1981 he commissioned Nicholas Grimshaw to build a new, high-tech Vitra factory and to produce a masterplan for the whole Vitra site.

Fehlbaum commissioned Frank Gehry's first building in Europe, a chair museum that was to become the Vitra Design Museum (1989). A second Gehry building was the Vitra Atelier, completed in 2003. Fehlbaum is also behind the first European work by Tadao Ando (a small conference centre dug into the ground, completed in 1993), who designs inspirationally calm buildings in concrete. Both Gehry and Ando went on to win the prestigious Pritzker Prize. Zaha Hadid, another Pritzker winner, also owes a great deal to Fehlbaum: he commissioned her first building, a fire station completed in 1993, at a time when everyone else thought her drawings were beautiful but

impossibly unworkable. Fehlbaum's architectural talent-spotting means that the Vitra factory site now contains more important contemporary buildings than many major cities. Most of these buildings were commissioned before the architects were famous, through the foresight of one thoughtful and unassuming man.

The Vitra campus also features a geodesic dome designed by Buckminster Fuller in 1978 and built in 2000; a petrol station designed by Jean Prouvé in 1959 and built in 2003; a factory building by Álvaro Siza, completed in 1984; VitraHaus, a visitor centre by Herzog & de Meuron, completed in 2010; and a further factory building by SANAA, also completed in 2010.

As a company, Vitra gave to the RIBA the furniture for the study rooms at the Victoria and Albert Museum, and is responsible for the touring Le Corbusier exhibition of 2008–09 that the RIBA Trust staged in Liverpool and, jointly with the Barbican, in London.

COLIN HAYWARD
QUANTITY SURVEYOR AND CONSULTANT FOR KMCS

Colin Hayward is a consultant for KMCS and has experience in cost consultation for education and community-regeneration projects, arts projects, including major galleries and theatres, public exhibitions, dance and music venues, and nursery accommodation. He is an enabler for the Commission for Architecture and the Built Environment (CABE), offering advice and support to organizations commissioning buildings and public spaces.

For many years Hayward was a partner at Boyden's quantity surveyors, where he worked on Ron Herron's Imagination building on Store Street, London (1990), and with such leading architects as Eva Jiricna and Fletcher Priest. Projects on which he was quantity surveyor include Ellis Williams's Baltic Centre for Contemporary Art in Gateshead (2002) and the New Art Gallery Walsall by Caruso St John Architects (2000). More recently he worked with KMCS as cost consultant to such architects as Keith Williams, Ian Simpson and Glen Howells.

In architect Peter Cook's words, Hayward 'is a quantity surveyor who has commended himself to generations of architects through his total professionalism, which has been accompanied by an uncanny knack for seeing past the limitations of cost and efficiency, to the essence of architecture. Hayward understands people and motives; he understands the value that can be placed upon intelligent solutions that prioritize certain techniques or materials that others would just regard as quirky or tiresome.'

Hayward supports not only young architects but also artistic endeavours, most recently Tonkin Liu's (RIBA National Award-winning) 'Singing Ringing Tree' project (2006) on the Lancashire moors.

Client David Rosenberg speaks for all Hayward's clients when he says: 'Colin not only promotes design far beyond any other QS I have encountered, or with whom I have worked, but also appears happy at all times to act as mentor and adviser, and to give his all when less might be paid for.'

HANS-ULRICH OBRIST
CURATOR AND ART CRITIC

Hans-Ulrich Obrist, a Swiss, was born in Zurich. In 1993 he founded the Museum Robert Walser as a 'museum on the move'. The idea was to establish a non-monumental, 'elastic' institution in which 'every exhibition should be like the first time'. In Paris he ran the Migrateurs programme, a series of interventions by young artists, including noise musician Masami Akita (aka Merzbow), at the Musée d'Art Moderne de la Ville de Paris. During his time there as Curator of Contemporary Art he also co-curated exhibitions on the work of Olafur Eliasson, Philippe Parreno, Steve McQueen, Jonas Mekas and Yoko Ono.

Obrist has since curated *Manifesta 1*, the first edition of the roving European biennial of contemporary art (1996); *Cities on the Move* in Vienna, Bordeaux and London's Hayward Gallery (1999); *Retrace Your Steps: Remember Tomorrow* at the Sir John Soane Museum in London (1999–2000); *Mutations: Évènement culturel sur la ville contemporaine* (with Rem Koolhaas) in Bordeaux (2000–01); *The Air is Blue* at Luis Barragán House, Mexico City

(2002–03); and *Utopia Station* at the Venice Biennale of 2003 and in Munich (2004).

Obrist presently serves as Co-director of Exhibitions and Programmes and Director of International Projects at the Serpentine Gallery, London, working with the gallery's director, Julia Peyton-Jones, on the annual programme of temporary structures by internationally acclaimed architects and designers. The architects and artists who have been commissioned so far are: Zaha Hadid (2000); Daniel Libeskind with Arup (2001); Toyo Ito with Arup (2002); Oscar Niemeyer (2003); Álvaro Siza and Eduardo Souto de Moura with Cecil Balmond and Arup (2005); Rem Koolhaas and Cecil Balmond with Arup (2006); Olafur Eliasson and Kjetil Thorsen (2007); Frank Gehry (2008); SANAA (2009); Jean Nouvel (2010). The immediacy of the process – a maximum of six months from invitation to completion – provides a peerless model for commissioning architecture.

LIZ PEACE
CLIENT AND CHIEF EXECUTIVE OF THE
BRITISH PROPERTY FEDERATION

Liz Peace CBE is Chief Executive of the British Property Federation (BPF), a trade association with more than 400 corporate members and assets worth over £200 billion, which represents the interests of the commercial property industry in the UK. At the BPF, Peace has overhauled the strategy to produce a corporate plan aimed at raising the profile of the British property industry among politicians and other key stakeholders. She has also established strong links with the Treasury, communities and local government, and HM Revenue & Customs. Until recently she was a non-executive director of the Planning Inspectorate.

Peace began her career as a civil servant with the Ministry of Defence. During the 1990s she was a key player in the team that set up the Defence Evaluation and Research Agency and initiated its privatization.

Peace has become a well-known figure in the property industry since her appointment at

the BPF in 2002. Armed with a remit to raise the industry's profile in the eyes of government, she has done much to persuade it that the commercial property industry should be taken seriously as a means of delivering social and economic improvement. She counts among her campaign successes a string of improvements to planned legislation and regulation in the areas of taxation and planning, and the government's decision not to intervene with legislation on commercial leases; most recently, she has had the leadership of a pan-industry alliance that has persuaded the government to introduce Real Estate Investment Trusts.

Peace was awarded a CBE in 2008, for services to the property industry. She is a member of the Peabody Housing Trust's property committee, a trustee of LandAid, a non-executive director of Turley Associates and Chair of the European Property Federation's managing committee.

BRETT STEELE
DIRECTOR OF THE ARCHITECTURAL ASSOCIATION

Brett Steele is Director of the Architectural Association School of Architecture and of AA Publications in London. His contribution to the architectural community in the UK and internationally has been to take the heritage of the Architectural Association as one of the world's oldest schools of architecture and advance its role as a leader in architectural education; the school has a yearly enrolment of over 500 full-time students from more than sixty countries. Steele also directs the AA Public Programme, which organizes the world's largest series of public events dedicated to contemporary architectural culture. The programme includes visiting architects, artists, scholars and critics; exhibitions; symposia; and other events in London and abroad.

Steele's greatest contribution is as founder and former director of the AA's experimental Design Research Lab (AADRL), the innovative team- and network-based M.Arch programme at the cutting edge of architecture. He is also a partner of DAL, desArchLab, an architectural office in London.

Steele has taught and lectured worldwide, and is published widely. He was the editor of *Negotiate My Boundary* (2002), *Corporate Fields* (2005), *D[R]L Research* (2005) and *Supercritical* (2008), and edits the series *AA Words: Critical Thinking in Contemporary Architecture*. His articles, interviews and lectures have appeared in such publications as *Archis*, *Architectural Review*, *Harvard Design Magazine*, *The Architects' Journal*, *Japan Architect*, *Icon* and *Daidalos*, and on the BBC and CNN. Steele's particular interests include contemporary architecture and cities, architectural culture, and the impact on architectural education of new media and network-based design and communication systems.

The award of an honorary fellowship constitutes professional recognition of Steele's contribution to architecture in the UK and internationally.

ALBERT WILLIAMSON TAYLOR
ENGINEER AT ADAMS KARA TAYLOR

Albert Williamson Taylor is one of the founding partners of Adams Kara Taylor (AKT), the design-led structural and civil engineering consultancy. Its work includes visionary architecture, advanced geometry, sustainability, new technologies and civil engineering projects. The firm strives to develop innovative, environmentally friendly solutions that reduce negative impacts by reducing the consumption of non-renewable resources and minimizing the waste associated with the construction industry.

AKT has the reputation of being one of the most forward-thinking engineering practices in the industry. The office is made up of small, flexible groups in order to ensure that newly recruited graduates are supervised by experienced engineers.

Before founding AKT in 1995 with Robin Adams and Hanif Kara, Taylor worked with Tony Hunt as the engineer in charge of the Sackler Galleries at London's Royal Academy of Arts (1991). AKT (which is now part of the White Young Green Group but retains its own identity) has an annual turnover of about £8 million. Its major projects include the 2000 Stirling Prize-winning Peckham Library by Will Alsop (2000); Zaha Hadid's Phaeno Science Centre in Germany (2005), shortlisted for the 2006 Stirling Prize; and Allford Hall Monaghan Morris's Yellow Building (2008), which won the 2009 Building Controls Industry Association's Building of the Year Award and was longlisted for the RIBA Stirling Prize.

AKT has successfully cut a design-led route through the market, and has developed a culture that challenges the norm, attacks complacency and encourages inquisitiveness. Taylor's contribution invariably makes a real difference to the qualitative outcome of the design process, the difference that marks out a project as exceptional. His input animates, opens up and inspires the design team, making each member ask for more from themselves and the project, so that greater synthesis is achieved and holistic value pushed to the fore.

THE RIBA PRESIDENT'S MEDALS STUDENT AWARDS

The RIBA has been awarding the President's Silver Medal since the 1850s. The President's Medals, in their current format, were established in 1984 and are regarded as an international benchmark for excellence in education. The aim of these prestigious awards is to promote excellence in the study of architecture, to reward talent and to encourage architectural debate worldwide. Each year students from schools of architecture in the United Kingdom and abroad aspire to be selected by their school to enter for the medals, and for the opportunity for their work to be recognized and publicly exhibited.

The President's Medals website (presidentsmedals.com) features all the nominations since 1998. On the site, which includes a database of projects and statements of intent from the students, schools define their educational policy and aims; tutors justify their nominations; and the judging panels explain their decision-making process.

Each year, the judging panels select up to twenty projects that receive awards. Medals are awarded in three categories: the Bronze Medal, for best design project at Part 1; the Silver Medal, for best design project at Part 2; and the Dissertation Medal. In addition, there is a maximum of three commendations in each category.

The winners of the 2009 awards received their medals and commendations in front of an audience of more than four hundred people at a prestigious ceremony held at the RIBA on 2 December. Previous guest speakers at the event have included Norman Foster, Alex James, Mark Lawson, Richard MacCormac, Richard Rogers, Martha Schwartz and Paul Smith.

An exhibition of entries was on display at the RIBA headquarters during December 2009 and January 2010, and in Liverpool, at the milkandsugar gallery, between February and April 2010.

Chaired by Oliver Richards (ORMS and RIBA Vice-President for Education), the judging panel for the design projects comprised Willem Jan Neutelings (Neutelings Riedijk Architects, Rotterdam), Eric Parry (Eric Parry Architects, London) and Nanako Umemoto (Reiser + Umemoto, New York). The jury for the Dissertation Medal, chaired by Professor Peter Blundell Jones (University of Sheffield), comprised Dr Tim Martin (De Montfort University), Professor Alan Powers (University of Greenwich) and Dr Alexandra Stara (Kingston University).

Wen Ying Teh from the Architectural Association won the Bronze Medal for her project 'An Augmented Ecology of Wildlife and Industry', and Nicholas Szczepaniak, from the University of Westminster, won the Silver Medal for his project 'A Defensive Architecture'. Rebecca Gregory from the University of Westminster won the Dissertation Medal for her work 'The Art of Skew Bridges: The Technique and Its History Explored'.

Atkins is the principal sponsor of the President's Medals. In 2009 the awards were also sponsored by the Institute of Materials, Minerals and Mining (IOM3), Service Point, the SOM Foundation and Ibstock Brick; *Architects' Journal* was the media partner.

An Augmented Ecology of Wildlife and Industry

A Defensive Architecture

The Art of Skew Bridges

BRONZE MEDAL

AN AUGMENTED ECOLOGY OF WILDLIFE AND INDUSTRY

WEN YING TEH
ARCHITECTURAL ASSOCIATION

A salt mine scars the landscape of the Galapagos Islands. Once the natural habitat of flamingos, this salt lake has long been a desolate space ravaged by the nearby restaurant industry. It is a symptom of the tension between the islands' enormous contribution to the Ecuadorian economy and their value as a historic wilderness.

This project is intended to provoke speculation on how these two demands may be reconciled as an alternative to the typical conservationist practices applied across the islands. The two traditionally mutually exclusive programmes of salt farming and flamingo habitat are re-imagined as a new form of symbiotic, designed ecology; a pink wonderland, built from coloured bacteria and salt crystallization, dissolving and reshaping itself with seasonal and evaporative cycles. The building becomes an ecosystem in itself, embedded in its context.

Formed from fine webs of nylon fibres held in an aluminium frame, this strange stringed instrument allows the salt-farming process to be drawn up out of the lake, returning the water to the endemic flamingos while ensuring that a vital local industry can continue. Using only capillary action, salt water from the lake crystallizes on the tensioned strings, forming glistening, translucent enclosures. It encrusts the infrastructure of a flamingo observation hide and solidifies into a harvestable field, ready to be scraped off by miners.

The project was developed through scale models that were used as host structures for an in-depth series of crystallization experiments. Material erosion, spatial qualities, structural capacity and evaporative cycles were all determined through physical testing. The architecture and its models grew slowly, emerging from the salt water in which they were immersed to become fully developed crystalline structures.

The ecology of the Galapagos Islands is in crisis. This project is positioned as part documentary, part science fiction, offering both a rigorous technical study and a speculative near-future wilderness. An evolving future for the islands is imagined, and it demands an evolved and mutated architecture.

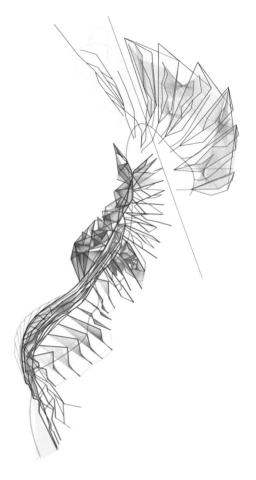

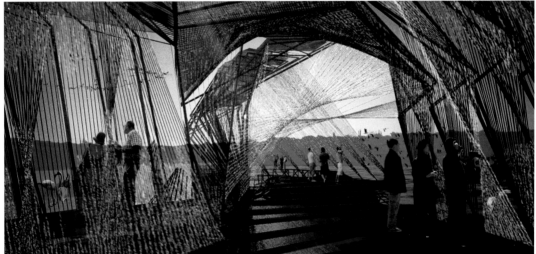

DW G... Ten Towers in Context

A DEFENSIVE ARCHITECTURE

NICHOLAS SZCZEPANIAK
UNIVERSITY OF WESTMINSTER

This project is intended to conjure unexpected readings of the built environment in the future if we fail to take more drastic steps to deal with climate change now. If the planet is left to change as it is currently doing, it is easy to imagine that soon fossil fuels will become scarce, and vast amounts of land will be lost because of rising water levels or arid climates.

Inevitably this change will have an undesired effect on social order and the built environment. Resources will have to be rationed, and public space will be further militarized in order to maintain social order. This will enhance an already emerging sense of inertia in public space. The idea of this project is to comment on and alert us to these problems.

THE ART OF SKEW BRIDGES:
THE TECHNIQUE AND ITS HISTORY EXPLORED

REBECCA GREGORY
UNIVERSITY OF WESTMINSTER

In the nineteenth century, as the railway advanced across the United Kingdom, bridges became an increasingly essential part of the industrial landscape. Despite the wider use of such materials as cast iron, many were still constructed of brick and stone.

The masonry-arch bridge is a relatively simple structure when two systems cross at ninety degrees to each other; however, it is not so easy when the systems cross at an oblique angle. This problem had previously been encountered in the design of canals, but it occurred more regularly with the railway. The long, sweeping curves of the railway line caused additional complexity, by contrast with the predominantly straight road and canal layouts. The solution to this problem was the skew or oblique bridge.

This may sound like a reasonably simple solution, and a relatively insignificant piece of civil engineering, but when one attempts to visualize a masonry arch bridge and to consider how the stonework may be skewed to allow for the oblique angle, the complexity quickly becomes apparent. This study looks in detail at one particular solution to the nineteenth-century problem of the skew bridge. It is based on a drawing published in *The Builder* in 1845 to accompany an article on the construction of skew bridges. An attempt is made here to explain this drawing fully and to investigate the circumstances surrounding its publication.

The dissertation concentrates on one particular drawing, but that serves as an example of the way the knowledge of descriptive geometry, derived from French military engineering, was adapted by British architects and engineers. The dissertation also considers the way such nineteenth-century civil-engineering structures as bridges were inevitably appropriated by the champions of British modernism in their search for a functionalist tradition. But also, focusing on the working relationship of two relatively unknown architects, the research reveals something of their individual professional lives and their place in history.

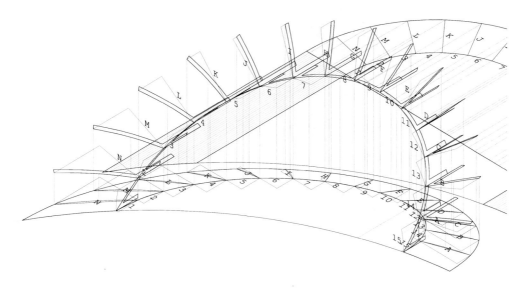

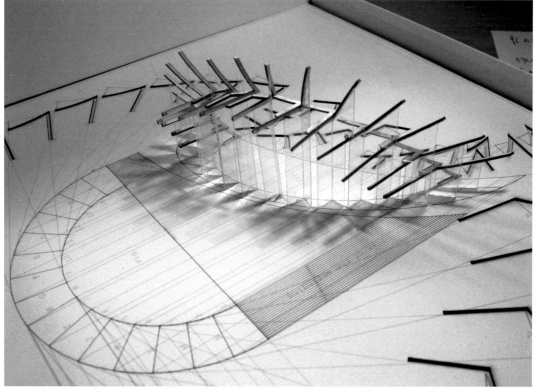

THE HOUSING DESIGN AWARDS

In 2010, sixty-two years after the Housing Design Awards were launched by Health Minister Nye Bevan, the Department of Health made a welcome return as a partner. A special award will be presented annually for a scheme that offers a more attractive option for housing our ageing population. Also in 2010, the Royal Institution of Chartered Surveyors, the housing industry's largest professional body, became a partner. This means that the awards represent a genuine cross-industry partnership between various arms of government, the private sector and all the professional institutions. Other new supporters are the London Development Agency (LDA) and its team at Design for London (DfL). With the addition of the new partners to the existing ones – Communities and Local Government (CLG), the RIBA, the National House-Building Council (NHBC), the Royal Town Planning Institute (RTPI) and the Homes and Communities Agency (HCA) – the Housing Design Awards are now uniquely judged by a large team of surveyors, architects and planners.

For their recent improvements, the awards owe a huge debt to Graham Pye, who chaired both the Sponsorship Committee and the judges from 1997 until his untimely death in June 2009. All those associated with the awards will miss his expertise and cross-industry commitment.

The new Chair is Gareth Capner, who is respected for turning architectural practice Barton Willmore into one of the largest planning and design consultancies in the country. His strong links with housebuilders and planners have already begun to strengthen the awards.

A new award was launched in 2010. Sponsored by CLG and supported by the Department of Health, it promotes some of the design ideas contained in the Housing an Ageing Population: Panel for Innovation (HAPPI) Report. The fact that millions of people now live active lives beyond retirement means that the twentieth-century default option of 'a quiet flat in a sheltered location' has been losing market share to secure city-centre apartments and clusters of interdependent dwellings around community hubs. Such schemes offer new opportunities to developers and consultants. When shaped in partnership with local authorities and communities, they can provide appropriate levels of care efficiently, and free up family houses occupied by single people by offering highly desirable new alternatives. The judges were delighted by the range of HAPPI schemes and made two awards, one for the best completed scheme and one for the best project.

The Housing Design Awards are made at two stages: for projects of great potential, where the scheme has detailed planning permission but is not yet finished and occupied; and for completed schemes of outstanding merit.

Developments may consist of private- or public-sector newbuild, conversion or renovation schemes in England, provided they contain four or more dwellings. Schemes that include non-residential elements may be entered, provided that housing constitutes a major part.

The awards are judged by a committee of representatives of CLG, RIBA, NHBC, RTPI, HCA, CABE, DfL/LDA, organized by David Birkbeck, Hon. FRIBA, and his team at Design for Homes. For each entry, the committee considers:

- relationship to surroundings and neighbourhood
- response to site constraints and opportunities
- layout, grouping and landscaping
- planning of roads and footpaths
- handling of garages and car parking
- attention to safety, security and accessibility
- external appearance and internal planning
- sustainability in construction
- finishes, detailing and workmanship

Entrants are also asked to assess themselves against 'Building for Life' criteria, which were developed by the Commission for Architecture and the Built Environment (CABE) in partnership with Design for Homes to measure urban design manners and public and private amenity in new housing.

hdawards.org

Icon, Street, Somerset

ICON
STREET, SOMERSET

FEILDEN CLEGG BRADLEY STUDIOS

DEVELOPER/CONTRACTOR: CREST NICHOLSON
PLANNING AUTHORITY: MENDIP DISTRICT COUNCIL
PUBLIC REALM ARCHITECT: GRANT ASSOCIATES
IMAGES: TIM CROCKER

Respect for climate and community was a feature of this year's overall winner. The scheme evolved through community workshops into an exceptional layout. The prime concerns of the design were traffic and loss of amenity, resulting in 40 per cent of the scheme being devoted to public open space, an existing local community at peace with the emerging new one, and some exceptional new houses.

The initial parcel of 138 homes suggests that the scheme will be the first real milestone in the evolution of layout, house and car-parking design since Poundbury, Dorset. As with that scheme, Icon's layout is driven by a philosophical desire to make it the place it was before cars. But at Street, any love of the past is strictly in keeping with the rhythm of its urbane neighbour, Bath, home to the scheme's architect. Long, straight boulevards run north–south, and terraces lead off at right angles to form the grid of a Georgian townscape.

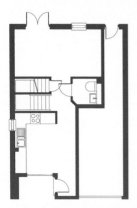 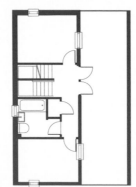

Typical ground-floor plan   Typical first-floor plan

Location plan

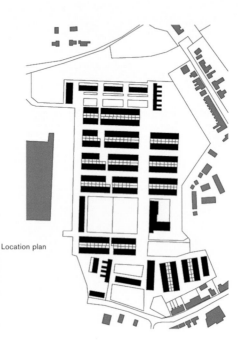

The scheme's origins coincided with guidance for spaces outside the home set out in the Department for Transport's *Manual for Streets*. What the publication preaches is so widely practised here that it could have been called the 'manual for Street'. Public squares, residential squares, boulevards, streets and mews are laid out in a hierarchy to manage traffic speed, and the change in character is supported by a lavish landscape of mature trees, tables, benches, planters and even topiary giraffes. Landscape architect Grant Associates has dressed these places as outdoor rooms.

Houses face each other in parallel terraces. The timber cladding gives the impression of a continuous frontage, but the party walls in the two-bedroom mews houses are in fact separated by a garage with deck above, overlooked by windows. The scheme accepts that in this part of the country people use cars, and makes a virtue of the need to garage them. The inhabitants can stop outside the front door to drop off their families before parking; the mews have additional remote parking. These integral house types achieve the perfect balance of garaging, urban design and daylighting to bedrooms and living spaces.

ARMOUR CLOSE
LONDON N7

HFI ARCHITECTS

DEVELOPER: HOMES FOR ISLINGTON
CONTRACTOR: MANSELL
PLANNING AUTHORITY: LONDON BOROUGH OF ISLINGTON
IMAGES: TIM CROCKER

London's Islington Council is building homes again, using its own money and land. Since 2007 its own newly hired architects have been producing feasibility studies for its land across the borough. There may be no greater challenge than this: a tiny former garages site between Pentonville Prison and a six-storey Victorian prison-officers' block.

The fronts of the four courtyard houses (which are designed for high environmental performance) rise to two storeys, and the monopitch roof rakes towards single-storey backs on the line of the mews. Daylighting is boosted with four lights in the roof pitch, two of which are remotely controlled and open for ventilation. When the clouds part, sunlight floods in.

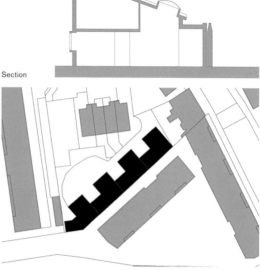

Section

Location plan

BARKING CENTRAL
LONDON IG11

ALLFORD HALL MONAGHAN MORRIS

DEVELOPER: REDROW REGENERATION
CONTRACTOR: ARDMORE CONSTRUCTION
PLANNING AUTHORITY: LONDON BOROUGH OF BARKING AND DAGENHAM
PUBLIC REALM ARCHITECT: MUF
IMAGES: TIM CROCKER

The creation of this scheme is reminiscent of an epic of a bygone age: heroic protagonists (private and public sector) sparking off each other for nine years against a backdrop of tumultuous market forces. The role of the local authority was fundamental to the emergence of a new town centre from the construction of 500 homes. A glorious conclusion is tinged with regret: we won't see the like again.

The landmark is the Lemonade Building, a seventeen-storey high-rise with small, competitively priced flats at the corners, enjoying the best views from recessed balconies. These are picked out in yellow and green in homage to R. White's lemonade, which was canned locally. The landscaping, too, is as bubbly as a can of pop.

Typical floor plans

Section

CLAREDALE STREET
LONDON E2

KARAKUSEVIC CARSON ARCHITECTS

DEVELOPER: TOWER HAMLETS COMMUNITY HOUSING
CONTRACTOR: HILL PARTNERSHIPS
PLANNING AUTHORITY: LONDON BOROUGH OF TOWER HAMLETS
IMAGES: TIM CROCKER

The scheme for seventy-seven dwellings next to Denys Lasdun's
Keeling House replaces his low-rise block with flats, a perimeter
block of two- and three-storey houses and another three-storey
terrace, apparently of town houses. In fact, many 'houses' in the
terrace have two doors to the street: one opens to a ground-floor
flat that wraps round a private courtyard with glazed walls; the other
opens to stairs, which lead up to a duplex flat.

All the buildings have green roofs with solar thermal panels for
hot water. The facing material is predominantly copper sheet, fixed
with an irregular pattern of joints that make it look handmade, in a
nod to the area's artisan history.

CONNAUGHT GARDENS
LONDON N10

POLLARD THOMAS EDWARDS ARCHITECTS

DEVELOPER: CONNAUGHT HOUSE DEVELOPMENTS
CONTRACTOR: ROOFF
PLANNING AUTHORITY: LONDON BOROUGH OF HARINGEY
IMAGES: TIM CROCKER

The villas of Muswell Hill enjoy dramatic views from the steep slopes. The balancing act for this newbuild scheme was to fulfil such potential while addressing neighbours' fears of being overlooked.

The terrace of seven houses exploits a steep fall between the street and the garden by tucking a floor below street level, planned as a large kitchen–diner, fully glazed to the garden for daylight. The glazed wall folds back for the perfect al fresco dining arrangement.

Windows to the second storey are the most constricted by the overlooking concern. On the top floor, slotted between the roof pitches, is an outdoor terrace big enough for a table, chairs, planters and even sun loungers.

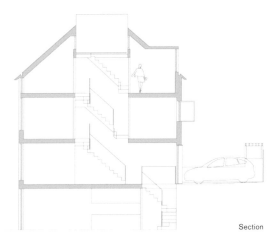

Section

MUSEUM COURT
LINCOLN

JONATHAN HENDRY ARCHITECTS

DEVELOPER: STRAIT DEVELOPMENT
CONTRACTOR: ROBERT WOODHEAD
PLANNING AUTHORITY: CITY OF LINCOLN COUNCIL
IMAGES: TIM CROCKER

This development of two restored houses and eighteen new flats
in the centre of Lincoln shows how to reproduce the finer points
of Georgian architecture in an honestly contemporary style. The
result is a terrace of six distinct buildings forming the north side
of a courtyard, with a seventh to the south. The terrace is unified
by the repetitive use of an upright rectangular window, Georgian in
proportion, with updated Georgian shutters expressed as a white-
painted MDF folding screen. These screens allow residents to shut
out light and noise without the window rhythm being lost to a tutti-
frutti of curtains and blinds. The flats are finished with oak floors
and bespoke joinery; those on the top floor have double-height
spaces with rooflights.

Elevation

HEALD FARM COURT
NEWTON-LE-WILLOWS

DKA

DEVELOPER: HELENA PARTNERSHIPS
CONTRACTOR: CRUDEN CONSTRUCTION
PLANNING AUTHORITY: ST HELENS COUNCIL
IMAGES: TIM CROCKER

This scheme has the crafted elegance of an Oxbridge quadrangle. Many of its eighty-six two-bedroom flats for market sale, rent and shared ownership are presented as terraces of gable-fronted villas. They are faced in a mixture of smart brickwork and bronzed copper cladding with dark powder-coated windows and generous balconies, and the detailing is consistently smart throughout.

The layout has to work for three distinct users: the visitor must feel welcome, the self-reliant resident should not feel institutionalized, and the more dependent should feel secure. The design achieves this by dividing flats into three blocks enveloping a services hub. The scheme is both heated and cooled by heat pumps feeding off ten deep-bore holes, and hot water is provided by a solar thermal system.

Typical floor plans

BUZZARDS MOUTH COURT
LONDON IG11

SHEPPARD ROBSON

DEVELOPER: BARKING RIVERSIDE
CONTRACTOR: TO BE APPOINTED
PLANNING AUTHORITY: LONDON BOROUGH OF BARKING AND DAGENHAM
IMAGES: HOUSING DESIGN AWARDS

Roughly half the first 1451 homes on this 150-hectare site on the north bank of the River Thames will have three or more bedrooms. One type is a three-storey town house, which – at 177 square metres – proudly exceeds by 50 per cent space standards recently championed by the Mayor. A second type is a 154-square-metre courtyard house with bedrooms stacked in a broad, shallow two-storey block. A third, three-bedroom type has a T-shaped plan so that both living space and master bedroom are dual aspect.

All houses are aligned so that the windows face east or west, to make the most of sunlight, and most have been designed to be fitted with a green roof.

Elevation

COMPSTALL MILLS
STOCKPORT

FEILDEN CLEGG BRADLEY STUDIOS

DEVELOPER: ASK DEVELOPMENTS
CONTRACTOR: TO BE APPOINTED
PLANNING AUTHORITY: STOCKPORT METROPOLITAN BOROUGH COUNCIL
IMAGES: HOUSING DESIGN AWARDS

This project involves the reinvention of a clutch of cotton mills dating from the 1820s. The river that once powered the mills will produce hydroelectric power to supply all the homes and offices. This power source, together with a gas-fired communal heating system, will make the 121-unit scheme one of the country's first large low-carbon developments, and the first retrofit eco-neighbourhood in a conservation area.

The shape and size of large mill buildings mean that divided flats typically have great floor-to-ceiling heights but tend to be single aspect. Here, clever manipulation of the section has resulted in more dual-aspect dwellings.

Newbuild elements include terraces of three- and four-bedroom houses with stairs leading up to a full-width roof terrace.

Riverhouse floor plans

DERWENTHORPE PHASE 1A
YORK

RICHARDS PARTINGTON ARCHITECTS

DEVELOPER: JOSEPH ROWNTREE HOUSING TRUST
CONTRACTOR: TO BE APPOINTED
PLANNING AUTHORITY: CITY OF YORK COUNCIL
IMAGES: HOUSING DESIGN AWARDS

The developer is none other than the Joseph Rowntree Housing
Trust, which built the exemplary New Earswick village scheme
in the same area at the beginning of the last century. This new
development owes a lot to that, reinterpreting Parker and Unwin's
Arts and Crafts style. The difference will be in the scheme's energy
footprint. Besides putting people as close as possible to work and
leisure, to cut travel, the development will include sixty-one homes
built to the Code Level 4. The remaining three homes will achieve
higher levels of the Code. With the prototypes already built and
being monitored, the first phase of Derwenthorpe is set to become
an important step towards a low-carbon exemplar in this country.

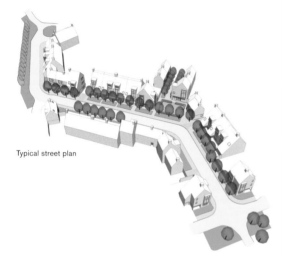

Typical street plan

THE LIBRARY BUILDING
LONDON SW4

STUDIO EGRET WEST

DEVELOPER: CATHEDRAL
CONTRACTOR: UNITED HOUSE
PLANNING AUTHORITY: LONDON BOROUGH OF LAMBETH
IMAGES: HOUSING DESIGN AWARDS

The proposals, which were preferred by both Lambeth Council
and design champions in Clapham's Civic Society in a limited
competition, take a corner site and let rip. Curved buildings of
seven to twelve storeys accommodating 136 market-sale flats,
some with 180-degree views, spin off a vortex that houses the
library. Here, the books are shelved on a ramp similar to the one at
the Greater London Authority headquarters – or even the Vatican.
The neighbourhood facilities are linked at ground-floor level with the
Primary Care Trust, which is tucked into the back of the site.

Joyous flourishes aside, the scheme promises to be highly
disciplined in its use of energy, with the ground-floor amenities built
to BREEAM 'Very Good' standard and the homes to Code Level 4.

Elevation

PEABODY AVENUE
LONDON SW1

HAWORTH TOMPKINS

DEVELOPER: PEABODY
CONTRACTOR: MANSELL
PLANNING AUTHORITY: WESTMINSTER CITY COUNCIL
IMAGES: HOUSING DESIGN AWARDS

It has taken the decades since the Blitz to repair the flaws created in the layout of Peabody Avenue by bomb damage, which destroyed four of the original twenty-six blocks. The new design has the massing and many of the materials of the original blocks, but is better. Innovations deal smartly with the weaknesses common to any tenement building. Flats along the railway line are pulled back behind corridor access, with balconies cantilevered towards the railway, screening the flats from rush-hour noise. The block turns east to create a double-height gated mouth, which allows a sense of ownership of the amenity spaces. One-third of the fifty-five new homes will be shared ownership, and all will be linked to the Pimlico district heating system.

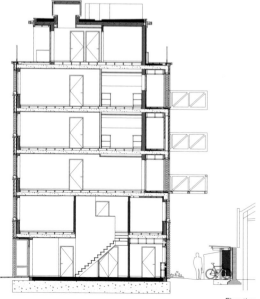

Elevation

SHIRECLIFFE
SHEFFIELD

STEPHENSON BELL ARCHITECTS

DEVELOPER: NORTH SHEFFIELD REGENERATION TEAM, SHEFFIELD CITY COUNCIL
CONTRACTOR: HENRY BOOT CONSTRUCTION
PLANNING AUTHORITY: SHEFFIELD CITY COUNCIL
IMAGES: HOUSING DESIGN AWARDS

Instead of decanting residents and temporarily housing them off-site while streets of homes are demolished and replaced, the aim is to scatter these new homes in little clusters throughout the predominantly council-owned estate. Just seventy-nine new units in sixteen pockets within 35 hectares of 1940s housing are expected to transform the residents' and outsiders' impression of the neighbourhood. By placing many units in visible locations, such as at road junctions, the council hopes to make the most impact for the smallest outlay.

The homes themselves will be built to Code Level 4 and will incorporate photovoltaic roof tiles in their simple roof pitches. With many councils – and the Treasury – watching, this project is one of the most important in the country.

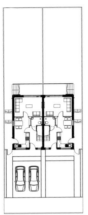

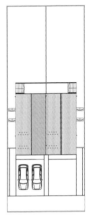

Typical floor plans

THE TRIANGLE
SWINDON

GLENN HOWELLS ARCHITECTS

DEVELOPER: HAB OAKUS
CONTRACTOR: WILLMOTT DIXON
PLANNING AUTHORITY: SWINDON BOROUGH COUNCIL
IMAGES: HOUSING DESIGN AWARDS

Hab Oakus is the development vehicle of Kevin McCloud, the television presenter who made drama out of self-build. Now he is putting his money where his mouth has been with this crack at speculative development. Hab's first forty-two homes will be mostly for rent in a scheme jointly developed by GreenSquare, and – naturally – their development is being filmed.

Houses will be built to Code Level 4 with triple glazing, air-source heat pumps and grey-water recycling. External walls will be built in hempcrete and a passive stack ventilation system will drive hot, stale air up the stairwell and out through a chimney. Ventilation cowls have become a motif of high-profile eco-schemes, but they were never as elegant as these.

Location plan

KIDBROOKE EXTRA CARE HOUSING
LONDON SE3

PRP ARCHITECTS

DEVELOPER/CONTRACTOR: BERKELEY
PLANNING AUTHORITY: LONDON BOROUGH OF GREENWICH
IMAGES: HOUSING DESIGN AWARDS

The layout of these 170 flats will foster discrete communities of neighbours who will more easily get to know one another. Flats cluster around five access cores, which are naturally lit and offer a quiet lounge and a large communal balcony on each level. The arrangement also maximizes the number of flats with more than one aspect.

At 70–84 square metres, the flats trounce expectations. Most have three habitable rooms, with the flexible third for use as a bedroom (for a carer or visitor), a study or a dining space, thanks to a sliding partition. All have a balcony or terrace big enough to accommodate a table, chairs and plants, helping to maximize exposure to direct sunlight and its benefits for ageing minds and bodies.

PREVIOUS WINNERS AND ROYAL GOLD MEDALLISTS

THE RIBA STIRLING PRIZE

1996   Hodder Associates, University of Salford

1997   Michael Wilford and Partners, Music School, Stuttgart

1998   Foster + Partners, American Air Museum, Duxford

1999   Future Systems, NatWest Media Centre, Lord's, London

2000   Alsop & Störmer, Peckham Library and Media Centre, London

2001   Wilkinson Eyre Architects, Magna, Rotherham

2002   Wilkinson Eyre Architects, Millennium Bridge, Gateshead

2003   Herzog & de Meuron, Laban, London

2004   Foster + Partners, 30 St Mary Axe, London

2005   EMBT/RMJM, The Scottish Parliament, Edinburgh

2006   Richard Rogers Partnership with Estudio Lamela, New Area Terminal, Barajas Airport, Madrid

2007   David Chipperfield Architects, Museum of Modern Literature, Marbach am Neckar

2008   Feilden Clegg Bradley Studios, Alison Brooks Architects, Maccreanor Lavington, Accordia, Cambridge

2009   Rogers Stirk Harbour + Partners, Maggie's London

THE RIBA LUBETKIN PRIZE

2006   Noero Wolff Architects, Red Location Museum of the People's Struggle, New Brighton, South Africa

2007   Grimshaw (Grimshaw Jackson Joint Venture), Southern Cross Station, Melbourne, Australia

2008   Gianni Botsford Architects, Casa Kike, Cahuita, Costa Rica

2009   Herzog & de Meuron, The National Stadium, Beijing

THE ARCHITECTS' JOURNAL FIRST BUILDING AWARD

2001   Walker Architecture, Cedar House, Logiealmond, Scotland

2002   Sutherland Hussey Architects, Barnhouse, London

2003   dRMM, No. 1 Centaur Street, London

2004   Annalie Riches, Silvia Ullmayer and Barti Garibaldo, In Between, London

2005   Amin Taha Architects, Gazzano House, London

THE RIBA MANSER MEDAL

2001   Cezary Bednarski, Merthyr Terrace, London

2002   Burd Haward Marston Architects, Brooke Coombes House, London

2003   Jamie Fobert Architects, Anderson House, London

2004   Mole Architects, Black House, Cambridgeshire

2005   Robert Dye Associates, Stealth House, London

2006   Knox Bhavan Architects, Holly Barn, Norfolk

2007   Alison Brooks Architects, The Salt House, St Lawrence Bay

2008   Rogers Stirk Harbour + Partners, Oxley Woods, Milton Keynes

2009   Pitman Tozer Architects, Gap House, London

THE CROWN ESTATE CONSERVATION AWARD

1998   Peter Inskip + Peter Jenkins, Temple of Concord and Victory, Stowe

1999   Foster + Partners, Reichstag, Berlin

2000   Foster + Partners, JC Decaux UK Headquarters, Brentford

2001   Rick Mather Architects, Dulwich Picture Gallery, London

2002   Richard Murphy Architects with Simpson Brown Architects, Stirling Tolbooth, Scotland

2003   LDN Architects, Newhailes House, Musselburgh, Scotland

2004   HOK International, King's Library at the British Museum, London

2005   Avanti Architects, Isokon (Lawn Road) Apartments, London

2006   Dixon Jones with Purcell Miller Tritton, the National Gallery East Wing and Central Portico, London

2007   Alec French Architects, SS *Great Britain* and

Historic Dockyard, Bristol

2008   Alastair Lansley (for Union Railways),

St Pancras International, London

2009   Union North, The Midland Hotel, Morecambe

THE RIBA CLIENT OF THE YEAR

1998   Roland Paoletti: new Jubilee line stations, London

1999   MCC: buildings at Lord's Cricket Ground, London

2000   Foreign & Commonwealth Office: embassies around
the world

2001   Molendinar Park Housing Association, Glasgow:
buildings by various Scottish architects

2002   Urban Splash: regeneration in Manchesterand Liverpool

2003   City of Manchester: post-IRA-bomb projects

2004   Peabody Trust: RIBA Award-winning schemes

2005   Gateshead Council: art and architecture projects

2006   Royal Botanic Gardens: buildings at Kew and
Wakehurst Place

2007   Derwent London: 28 Dorset Square, London

2008   Coin Street Community Builders: Coin Street
Neighbourhood Centre, London

2009   Camden & Islington Community Solutions: Kentish Town
Health Centre, London; Grosvenor: Liverpool One
Masterplan; Kielder Partnership: Kielder Observatory,
Northumberland; Maggie's: Maggie's London; Parabola
Land: Kings Place, London; St Martin-in-the-Fields,
London

THE ADAPT TRUST ACCESS AWARD

2001   Avery Associates Architects, Royal Academy of
Dramatic Arts, London

2002   Malcolm Fraser Architects, Dance Base, Edinburgh

2003   Nicoll Russell Studios, The Space, Dundee College

THE RIBA INCLUSIVE DESIGN AWARD

2004   Arup Associates, City of Manchester Stadium

2005   Foster + Partners, Sage, Gateshead

2006   Adjaye/Associates, Idea Store, Whitechapel, London

2007   Patel Taylor, Portland College New Learning Centre,
Mansfield

THE RIBA CABE PUBLIC SPACE AWARD

2008   Gustafson Porter, Old Market Square,
Nottingham

2009   McDowell + Benedetti Architects, Castleford Bridge,
Castleford

THE RIBA SUSTAINABILITY AWARD

2000   Chetwood Associates, Sainsbury's, Greenwich, London

2001   Michael Hopkins and Partners, Jubilee Campus,
University of Nottingham

2002   Cottrell + Vermeulen Architecture, Cardboard Building,
Westborough Primary School, Westcliff-on-Sea

2003   Bill Dunster Architects, BedZED, Wallington

2004   Sarah Wigglesworth Architects, Stock Orchard Street,
London

2005   Associated Architects, Cobtun House, Worcester

2006   Feilden Clegg Bradley Architects, Heelis, Swindon

2007   Architype, Upper Twyford Barns, Hereford

2008   Denton Corker Marshall, Manchester Civil Justice
Centre

THE RIBA SORRELL FOUNDATION SCHOOLS AWARD

2007   Building Design Partnership, Marlowe Academy,
Ramsgate

2008   Allford Hall Monaghan Morris, Westminster Academy at
the Naim Dangoor Centre, London

2009   Penoyre & Prasad, The Minster School, Southwell

1998	Ian Ritchie Architects, Terrasson Cultural Greenhouse, France
1999	Munkenbeck + Marshall, Sculpture Gallery, Roche Court, near Salisbury
2000	Softroom Architects, Kielder Belvedere, Northumberland
2001	Richard Rose-Casemore, Hatherley Studio, Winchester
2002	Cottrell + Vermeulen Architecture, Cardboard Building, Westborough Primary School, Westcliff-on-Sea
2003	Gumuchdjian Architects, Think Tank, Skibbereen
2004	Simon Conder Associates, Vista, Dungeness
2005	Niall McLaughlin Architects, House at Clonakilty, County Cork
2006	Alison Brooks Architects, Wrap House, London
2007	David Sheppard Architects, Wooda, Crackington Haven
2008	John Pawson, The Sackler Crossing, Royal Botanic Gardens, Kew, Richmond
2009	Simon Conder Associates, El Ray, Dungeness

The Royal Gold Medal for the promotion of architecture, instituted by Queen Victoria in 1848, is conferred annually by the sovereign on some distinguished architect or group of architects for work of high merit, or on some distinguished person or group whose work has promoted either directly or indirectly the advancement of architecture.

1848	Charles Robert Cockerell, RA
1849	Luigi Canina, Italy
1850	Sir Charles Barry, RA
1851	Thomas L. Donaldson
1852	Leo von Klenze, Austria
1853	Sir Robert Smirke, RA
1854	Philip Hardwick, RA
1855	J.I. Hittorff, France
1856	Sir William Tite
1857	Owen Jones
1858	August Stuler, Germany
1859	Sir George Gilbert Scott, RA
1860	Sydney Smirke, RA
1861	J.B. Lesueur, France
1862	Revd Robert Willis
1863	Anthony Salvin
1864	E. Viollet-le-Duc, France
1865	Sir James Pennethorne
1866	Sir M. Digby Wyatt
1867	Charles Texier, France
1868	Sir Henry Layard
1869	C.R. Lepsius, Germany
1870	Benjamin Ferrey
1871	James Fergusson
1872	Baron von Schmidt, Austria
1873	Thomas Henry Wyatt
1874	George Edmund Street, RA
1875	Edmund Sharpe
1876	Joseph Louis Duc, France
1877	Charles Barry
1878	Alfred Waterhouse, RA
1879	Marquis de Vogue, France
1880	John L. Pearson, RA
1881	George Godwin

1882	Baron von Ferstel, Austria	1923	Sir John James Burnet, FRIAS, RA, RSA
1883	Francis Cranmer Penrose	1924	Not awarded
1884	William Butterfield	1925	Sir Giles Gilbert Scott, OM, DCL, RA
1885	H. Schliemann, Germany	1926	Professor Ragnar Östberg, Sweden
1886	Charles Garnier, France	1927	Sir Herbert Baker, KCIE, RA
1887	Ewan Christian	1928	Sir Guy Dawber, RA, FSA
1888	Baron von Hansen, Austria	1929	Victor Alexandre Frederic Laloux, France
1889	Sir Charles T. Newton	1930	Percy Scott Worthington, FSA
1890	John Gibson	1931	Sir Edwin Cooper, RA
1891	Sir Arthur Blomfield, ARA	1932	Dr Hendrik Petrus Berlage, The Netherlands
1892	César Daly, France		
1893	Richard Morris Hunt, USA	1933	Sir Charles Reed Peers, CBE, PPSA
1894	Lord Leighton, RA	1934	Henry Vaughan Lanchester, PPTPI
1895	James Brooks	1935	Willem Marinus Dudok, The Netherlands
1896	Sir Ernest George, RA	1936	Charles Henry Holden, MTPI
1897	Dr P.J.H. Cuypers, The Netherlands	1937	Sir Raymond Unwin
1898	George Aitchison, RA	1938	Professor Ivar Tengbom, Sweden
1899	George Frederick Bodley, RA	1939	Sir Percy Thomas, OBE, JP, MTPI
1900	Professor Rodolfo Amadeo Lanciani, Italy	1940	Charles Francis Annesley Voysey
1901	Not awarded, owing to the death of Queen Victoria	1941	Frank Lloyd Wright, USA
1902	Thomas Edward Collcutt	1942	William Curtis Green, RA
1903	Charles F. McKim, USA	1943	Professor Sir Charles Herbert Reilly, OBE
1904	Auguste Choisy, France	1944	Sir Edward Maufe, RA
1905	Sir Aston Webb, PPRA	1945	Victor Vessnin, USSR
1906	Sir L. Alma-Tadema, RA	1946	Professor Sir Patrick Abercrombie, FSA, PPTPI, FILA
1907	John Belcher, RA	1947	Professor Sir Albert Edward Richardson, RA, FSA
1908	Honoré Daumet, France	1948	Auguste Perret, France
1909	Sir Arthur John Evans, FRS, FSA	1949	Sir Howard Robertson, MC, ARA, SADG
1910	Sir Thomas Graham Jackson	1950	Eliel Saarinen, USA
1911	Wilhelm Dorpfeld, Germany	1951	Emanuel Vincent Harris, OBE, RA
1912	Basil Champneys	1952	George Grey Wornum
1913	Sir Reginald Blomfield, RA, FSA	1953	Le Corbusier (C.E. Jeanneret), France
1914	Jean Louis Pascal, France	1954	Sir Arthur George Stephenson, CMG, AMTPI, Australia
1915	Frank Darling, Canada	1955	John Murray Easton
1916	Sir Robert Rowand Anderson, FRIAS	1956	Dr Walter Adolf Georg Gropius, USA
1917	Henri Paul Nenot, Membre de l'Institut, France	1957	Hugo Alvar Henrik Aalto, Finland
1918	Ernest Newton, RA	1958	Robert Schofield Morris, FRAIC, Canada
1919	Leonard Stokes	1959	Professor Ludwig Mies van der Rohe, USA
1920	Charles Louis Girault, Membre de l'Institut, France	1960	Professor Pier Luigi Nervi, Italy
1921	Sir Edwin Landseer Lutyens, OM, KCIE, RA, FSA	1961	Lewis Mumford, USA
1922	Thomas Hastings, USA	1962	Professor Sven Gottfried Markelius, Sweden

1963	Lord Holford, ARA, PPTPI, FILA	2002	Archigram
1964	E. Maxwell Fry, CBE	2003	Rafael Moneo, Spain
1965	Professor Kenzo Tange, Japan	2004	Rem Koolhaas, The Netherlands
1966	Ove Arup, CBE, MICE, MIStructE	2005	Frei Otto, Germany
1967	Sir Nikolaus Pevsner, CBE, FBA, FSA, Hon ARIBA	2006	Toyo Ito, Japan
1968	Dr Richard Buckminster Fuller, FRSA, Hon AIA, USA	2007	Jacques Herzog and Pierre de Meuron, Switzerland
		2008	Edward Cullinan, CBE
		2009	Álvaro Siza, Portugal
1969	Jack Antonio Coia, CBE, RSA, AMTPI, FRIAS	2010	I.M Pei, USA
1970	Professor Sir Robert Matthew, CBE, ARSA, FRIAS		

1971   Hubert de Cronin Hastings

1972   Louis I. Kahn, USA

1973   Sir Leslie Martin

1974   Powell & Moya

1975   Michael Scott, Ireland

1976   Sir John Summerson, CBE, FBA, FSA

1977   Sir Denys Lasdun, CBE

1978   Jørn Utzon, Denmark

1979   The Office of Charles and Ray Eames, USA

1980   James Stirling

1981   Sir Philip Dowson, CBE

1982   Berthold Lubetkin

1983   Sir Norman Foster

1984   Charles Correa, India

1985   Sir Richard Rogers

1986   Arata Isozaki, Japan

1987   Ralph Erskine, CBE

1988   Richard Meier, USA

1989   Renzo Piano, Italy

1990   Aldo van Eyck, The Netherlands

1991   Colin Stansfield Smith, CBE

1992   Peter Rice, DIC(IC), MICE

1993   Giancarlo de Carlo, Italy

1994   Michael and Patricia Hopkins

1995   Colin Rowe, USA

1996   Harry Seidler, Australia

1997   Tadao Ando, Japan

1998   Oscar Niemeyer, Brazil

1999   The City of Barcelona, Spain

2000   Frank Gehry, USA

2001   Jean Nouvel, France

This list includes honorific tiles at the time of the award and professional but not academic qualifications.

SPONSORS

The RIBA is grateful to all the sponsors
who make the awards possible.

The *Architects' Journal* is the UK's leading architectural magazine.
It has been promoting good architecture since 1895. *AJ* believes
that the architectural profession benefits from having a single,
pre-eminent and undisputed award for quality design. That is why,
throughout its ten-year investment with the RIBA, the *Architects'
Journal* has helped the RIBA Stirling Prize to become recognized as
the highest achievement in UK architecture by both the profession
and the general public.

Kingspan Benchmark is a new architectural business from
Kingspan that provides a turning point in the way in which
inspirational architectural roof and façade systems can become a
reality. Developed to bring about change in architectural design, the
Benchmark product range is the result of comprehensive research,
partnership working and innovative thinking that will enable bold
new designs to be created from a wide variety of materials, colours
and textures without compromising on style and performance.

HSBC **Private Bank**

HSBC Private Bank is proud to partner with the RIBA as exclusive
sponsor of the RIBA Manser Medal. This new partnership builds on
the bank's long-established commitment to design while underlining
its respect for clients, architects and other professionals who create
inspiring houses through exceptional design. HSBC Private Bank
and the RIBA are leaders in their respective fields with a shared
commitment to excellence. HSBC Private Bank has unrivalled
property-lending expertise for private clients in the UK, as well as
providing expert advice for clients seeking outstanding homes.

THE CROWN ⬡ ESTATE

The Crown Estate is proud to sponsor the Crown Estate
Conservation Award. Now in its thirteenth year, this award is
presented for the work that best demonstrates the successful
restoration and/or conservation of an architecturally significant
building. The Crown Estate manages a large and uniquely diverse
portfolio of land and buildings across the UK. One of its primary
concerns is to make historic buildings suitable for today's users.

The Bloxham Charitable Trust

The first RIBA Client of the Year was named in 1998. The award
recognizes the role that good clients play in the delivery of fine
architecture. The fifth winner, in 2002, was Urban Splash, for
'its commitment both to design and quality and the regeneration
of Manchester and Liverpool'. Urban Splash's co-founder
Tom Bloxham now supports the award through the Bloxham
Charitable Trust.

The Commission for Architecture and the Built Environment (CABE)
is sponsor of the Public Space Award. CABE is the government's
adviser on architecture, urban design and public space. The Public
Space Award demonstrates that public spaces are as important as
housing, schools, offices or any other buildings because the public
use such spaces far more than they do buildings. We know that the
public see the value in quality spaces and the difference they can
make to their lives. The aim of the award is to encourage dialogue
and co-operation across professions and to recognize the
important role of landscape architects and urban designers in the
process of creating places.

The Sorrell Foundation was set up in 1999 to inspire creativity in young people and to improve quality of life through good design. In its fourth year, the RIBA Sorrell Foundation Schools Award continues to raise further the standard of design in all new primary- and secondary-school buildings and to reward excellence in school architecture.

The Marco Goldschmied Foundation continues its thirteen-year-long support for the Stephen Lawrence Prize, established in memory of the murdered teenager who aspired to be an architect. The Foundation provides the £5000 prize money and funds a £10,000 Stephen Lawrence Scholarship at the Architectural Association.

RIBA Award plaques are produced and donated by the Lead Sheet Association (LSA). The LSA is the primary independent body involved in the promotion and development of the use of rolled-lead sheet. The LSA is proud to have been associated with the RIBA Awards since 1989.

Ibstock is the UK's largest brickmaker, and its products provide beauty and protection for many leading buildings. Ibstock has a long association with architecture and especially the RIBA. This partnership has led to sponsorship of many of the local awards schemes run by the RIBA regions. Ibstock's commitment to the architectural profession runs much deeper, however, with support for the RIBA Student Newsletter and the RIBA Stirling Prize, as well as support for international study tours and lecture programmes at many of the leading schools of architecture.

NBS

A good specification is critical to the success of a building project, and an essential, integral part of the design process. For more than thirty-five years, UK architects have turned to National Building Specification master specification systems to produce technically robust, up-to-date project specifications. NBS also offers software for efficient contract administration, online and offline solutions to provide access to technical and regulatory information, and a range of learning services to keep construction professionals' skills and knowledge current. NBS is part of RIBA Enterprises, the commercial arm of the RIBA.

The RIBA would like to thank all the awards judges, who give freely of their time and whose reports form the basis of much of the text of this book.

The RIBA also thanks the photographers whose work is published in this book (credits appear in the individual entries or on p. 271) and who agreed to waive copyright fees for the reproduction of their work in connection with the RIBA's promotion of the awards.

INDEX